The Law

AUSTRALIA
LBC Information Services
Sydney

CANADA AND THE USA
Carswell

NEW ZEALAND
Brooker's
Auckland

SINGAPORE AND MALAYSIA
Thomson Information (S.E. Asia)
Singapore

The Law of Meetings

Michael Maloney and Jarlath Spellman

ROUND HALL SWEET & MAXWELL
DUBLIN
1999

Published in 1999 by
Round Hall Sweet & Maxwell
Brehon House, 4 Upper Ormond Quay
Dublin 7

Typeset by
AME Typesetting & Design

Printed by
Genprint, Dublin

ISBN 1-899738-62 2

A catalogue record for this book
is available from the British Library.

Table of Contents

Table of Cases

IRISH CONSTITUTION

Bunreacht na hEireann 1937

PRE-1922 STATUTES

POST-1922 IRISH STATUTES

STATUTORY INSTRUMENTS

EUROPEAN LEGISLATION

TABLE OF CASES

PRE-1922

RULINGS OF ENGLISH COURTS SINCE 1922

Foreword

Life – and law – grow ever more complicated. The increasing complexity of our society has led inevitably to a vast increase in the number of groups and alliances. Residents' associations, lobbying organisations and special interest groups of all types are an integral and essential part of modern society. Huge numbers of people involved in activities – from aerobics to zoology – spend a great deal of time at meetings of one kind or another. Our business and leisure activities are hugely affected by meetings. We are social and political animals.

In recent years the relentless growth of judicial review is a striking development in Irish law. It has profound implications for those conducting meetings and making decisions at them. Welcome or not, this is not likely to change in the foreseeable future. We are litigious creatures.

In this context, the publication of *The Law of Meetings* is timely indeed. It is the first textbook of its type dealing specifically with Irish law. The position here differs considerably from neighbouring jurisdictions, not only because of the differences in legislation, but because of the development of Irish constitutional law concerning natural and constitutional justice.

This book by two practising barristers, therefore, fills a gap in Irish legal literature. It is likely to become the standard reference book on the subject. The style is simple and unadorned, and the book is more valuable for that. It is refreshingly free of jargon. It will be of use not only to legal practitioners but to administrators, company secretaries, business people and politicians – actual or prospective – local or national. Perhaps it also could prove useful for teachers of civics charged with the education of the next generation of meeting organisers and attenders.

I congratulate the authors, warmly welcome the publication of this book and wish it every success.

Kevin C. O'Higgins
Judge of the High Court
The Four Courts
Dublin 7

Preface

This book has been written to cater for the needs of those associated with meetings in any capacity. It is also intended for anyone who wishes to become specifically acquainted with the law governing meetings in the Republic of Ireland.

The initiative for this book was inspired in part by the fact that there was a dearth of material on this subject and reliance had to be placed primarily on English texts such as the classic work, *Shackleton on the Law and Practice of Meetings.*

However, it has to be borne in mind that there is a significant divergence between the laws of the two jurisdictions on such matters as company meetings, meetings of the Houses of the Oireachtas, natural justice and public meetings, including the Criminal Justice (Public Order) Act 1994.

We thank Mr Justice Kevin O'Higgins for his foreword. His comments are much appreciated.

There are of course many people we would like to thank for their assistance in the writing of this book. In particular, we thank Mr Seamus Sorohan S.C., Mr Joseph Maloney, Lecturer in Accountancy at DIT, Mr Bernard Dunleavy B.L. for research in the area of company law and meetings and Ms Maria Colbert B.L. for her help on Local Authority Committees. We are most grateful to Mr Patrick Keane MCC, Clare County Council, for providing information on standing orders and Local Authorities, and to the staff of the Law Library, especially Des Mulhare, Albert McDonald and Teddy O'Neill for their help in obtaining case citations.

We also express our gratitude to the staff at Round Hall Sweet & Maxwell, especially to Therese Carrick for commissioning the work, Selga Medenieks, Anne McEntee and, in particular, Kieran Lyons for helping us bring the book to publication.

Lastly, our heartfelt thanks to our wives and families for their patience and support.

Although we have made every effort to state the law as of July 1999, we cannot accept responsibility for any loss occasioned to anyone acting or refraining to act on the contents of this publication. Professional advice should always be sought when considering any legal action.

This book is dedicated to our mothers: the late Bridget Kelly Maloney and Philomena O'Sullivan Spellman.

Michael Maloney and Jarlath Spellman
Dublin
July 1999

Part One: Meetings in General

1. Introduction and Public Meetings

A concise definition of what constitutes a meeting is to be found at common law in the case of *Sharpe v. Dawes*[1] "An assembly of people for a lawful purpose..."

It follows from this definition that the participants attending a meeting must be present in the same place and at the same time. The definition espoused in *Sharpe v. Dawes* implies that there must be more than one person present if the meeting is to be valid, but if two individuals are in separate rooms which are connected by audio and/or visual contact, that will suffice to bring this type of contact within the definition of a meeting. The persons attending the meeting must be there for a purpose particular to all the participants.[1a]

In company law an exception to the rule that at least two persons are required to constitute a meeting arises in the case of a limited company where the shareholders hold all the shares in a limited company.[2]

The purpose of a meeting is generally achieved by facilitating the members to communicate their thoughts on the matters under discussion and reach a consensus on a given topic.

It is usually a prerequisite of a meeting that it be governed by its rules of procedure, if any, and that it be properly constituted. The word "lawful" denotes that a meeting must not be for a purpose forbidden by law. There are two types of meeting: public meetings and private meetings.

1. Public Meetings

These meetings are normally constituted to discuss matters of public interest and are not subject to the same predetermined regulations that would apply to a constituted body.

The public have a right to attend such meetings subject to the conditions, if any, imposed by relevant legislation and/or local authority by-

---

[1] *Sharpe v. Dawes* [1876] 2 Q.B.D.29

[1a] *Byng v London Life Assurance Ltd.* [1989] 2 W.L.R. 738

[2] See *European Communities (Single-Member Private Limited Companies)* S.1. 275/1994 which implemented Directive 89/667.

laws. A public meeting is usually held in a public place, but it also follows that such a meeting can be held on private premises.

If a public meeting is held on private premises, members of the public may attend provided that they comply with any rules or regulations stipulated by the organisers. However, it is more expedient for a public meeting to be held in a public place.

A useful definition of what constitutes a public place can be found in section 3 of the Criminal Justice (Public Order) Act 1994 which states:

"(a) any highway,
(b) any outdoor area to which at the material time members of the public have or are permitted to have access, whether as of right or as a trespasser or otherwise, and which is used for public recreational purposes,
(c) cemetery or churchyard,
(d) any premises or other place to which at the material time members of the public have or are permitted to have access, whether as of right or by express or implied permission, or whether on payment or otherwise, and
(e) any train, vessel or vehicles used for the carriage of persons for reward."

At common law there is no unfettered right to hold a meeting in a public place. It follows, however, that if a person joins others for that purpose, that individual has a right not to be removed, provided that he or she does not commit a breach of the peace[3] and complies with relevant statutory provisions and by-laws.[4]

Article 40.6.1°.ii of the Irish Constitution of 1937 recognises a right to hold a public meeting, but it follows from the wording that such a right is not absolute. It states:

"The State guarantees liberty for the exercise subject to public order and morality of the right of the citizen to assemble peaceably and without arms.Provision may be made by law to prevent or control

---

[3] See *R. v. Langley* 6 Mod 125.

[4] In *Hirst v. Chief Constable of West Yorkshire Police* (1986) J.P. 151, it was held that an interlocutory injunction would not be granted to interfere with the right to demonstrate any more than it would be to interfere with free speech, provided everything is "done peaceably and in good order".

meetings which are determined in accordance with law to be calculated to cause a breach of the peace or to be a danger or nuisance to the general public and to prevent or control meetings in the vicinity of either of the Oireachtas."

2. Statutory Provisions and the Law of Meetings

There are a number of statutory provisions restricting the holding of a public meeting. Section 28 of the Offences Against the State Act 1939 imposes restrictions on meetings held in the vicinity of either House of the Oireachtas. Section 28(1) states that:

"It shall not be lawful for any public meeting to be held in or any procession to pass along or through, any public street or unenclosed place which or any part of which is situate within one-half of a mile from any building in which both Houses or either House of the Oireachtas are or is sitting or about to sit if either –

(a)   an officer of the Gárda Síochána not below the rank of chief superintendent has, by notice given to a person concerned in the holding or organisation of such meeting or procession or published in a manner reasonably calculated to come to the knowledge of the persons so concerned prohibiting the holding of such meeting in or the passing of such procession along or through any such public street or unenclosed space as aforesaid; or

(b)   a member of the Gárda Síochána calls on the persons taking part in such meeting or procession to disperse."

Section 28(2)(a) states that:

"Every person who –

(a)   shall organise, hold, or take part in or attempt to organise, hold, or take part in a public meeting or a procession in any such public street or unenclosed place as is mentioned in the foregoing sub-section of this section after such meeting or procession has been prohibited by a notice under paragraph (a) of the said sub-section.

(b) shall hold or take part in or attempt to hold or take part in a public meeting or a profession in any such public street or unenclosed place as aforesaid after a member of the Gárda Síochána has, under paragraph (b) of the said sub-section called upon the persons taking part in such meeting or procession to disperse, or

(c) shall remain in or enter into any such public street or unen closed space after being called upon to disperse as aforesaid;

shall be guilty of an offence under this section and shall be liable on summary conviction thereof to a fine not exceeding fifty pounds, or at the discretion of the Court, to imprisonment for a term not exceeding three months or to both such fine and such imprisonment."

Section 27(1) states that:

"(1) It shall not be lawful to hold a public meeting which is held or purports to be held by or on behalf of or by arrangement or in concert with an unlawful organisation or which is held or purports to be held for the purpose of supporting, aiding, abetting, or encouraging an unlawful organisation or of advocating the support of an unlawful organisation.

(2) Whenever an officer of the Gárda Síochána not below the rank of chief superintendent is of opinion that the holding of a particular public meeting about to be or proposed to be held would be a contravention of the next preceding sub-section of this section, it shall be lawful for such officer by notice given to a person concerned in the holding or organisation of such meeting or published in a manner reasonably calculated to come to the knowledge of the persons so concerned, to prohibit the holding of such meeting, and thereupon the holding of such meeting shall become and be unlawful.

(3) Whenever an officer of the Gárda Síochána gives any such notice as is mentioned in the next preceding sub-section of this section, any person claiming to be aggrieved by such notice may apply to the High Court in a summary manner on notice to the Attorney-General for such order as is hereinafter mentioned

and, upon the hearing of such application, the High Court if it so thinks proper, may make an order annulling such notice.

(4) Every person who organises or holds or attempts to organise or hold a public meeting the holding of which is a contravention of this section or who takes part or is concerned in the organising or the holding of any such meeting shall be guilty of an offence under this section and shall be liable on summary conviction thereof to a fine not exceeding fifty pounds or, at the discretion of the Court, to imprisonment for a term not exceeding three months or to both such fine or such imprisonment."

There are statutory provisions governing meetings which obstruct the administration of justice pursuant to the Offences against the State (Amendment) Act 1972. Section 4(1) states that:

"(a) Any public statement made orally, in writing or otherwise or any meeting procession or demonstration in public that constitutes an interference with the course of justice shall be unlawful.

(b) A statement, meeting, procession or demonstration shall be deemed to constitute an interference with the course of justice if it is intended, or is of such a character as to be likely, directly or indirectly, to influence any Court, person or authority concerned with the institution, conduct or defence of any civil or criminal proceedings (including a party or witness) as to whether or how the proceedings should be instituted, conducted, continued or defended, or as to what should be their outcome.

(c) A person who makes any statement, or who organises, holds or takes part in any meeting, procession or demonstration that is unlawful under this section shall be guilty of an offence and shall be liable."

There are penalties provided for in section 4(2)(a) and (b) on summary or indictable conviction.

3. Interference with Political Meetings

This matter is dealt with under the Public Meetings Act 1908 which, to date, has not been repealed. Section 1 states that:

"(1) Any person who at a lawful public meeting acts in a disorderly manner for the purpose of preventing the transaction of the business for which the meeting is called to gather shall be guilty of an offence and if the offence at a political meeting held in any parliamentary constituency between date of issue of a writ for the return of a Member of Parliament for such constituency at the date at which a return of such writ is made, he shall be guilty of an illegal practice within the meaning of the Corrupt and Illegal Practice and Prevention Act 1883 and in any other case shall on summary conviction, be liable to a fine not exceeding £5 or to imprisonment not exceeding one month.

(2) Any person who incites others to commit an offence under this section shall be guilty of a like offence."[5]

Although this Act is relevant, it would appear that it has not been utilised in modern times. The question that could be posed at this stage is whether the effectiveness of the 1908 Act is superceded by the Criminal Justice (Public Order) Act 1994.

4. Meetings which Obstruct the Highway

At common law there is no absolute right to obstruct a highway and if such an obstruction occurs it may well constitute a public nuisance. But it does not necessarily follow that because a meeting is held on a highway it is unlawful.[6] The common law dictates that a highway can be used by members of the public for passing and repassing and purposes reasonably incidental thereto.[7]

---

[5] For a definition of an illegal practice under this Act see s.7(1) of the Corrupt and Illegal Practices Prevention Act 46 & 47 Vict. Vol. XIX 1863 at 245.

[6] *Burden v. Rigler* [1911] 1 K.B. 337.

[7] *Harrison v. Duke of Rutland* [1893] 1 K.B. 142.

5.   Definition of a Highway

A highway has been defined in the past as "...a passage which is open to all the King's subjects".[8] It has also been held that this right has been created by dedication to the public for the occupation of the surface of the land for passing and repassing and their obligation to repair.[9] A roadway can also be created by statutory authority.[10] A strip of waste ground adjoining the public highway was held not to form part of the highway in the absence of evidence to show any use by the public of the strip.[11] A highway has been held to be a path, road, bridge or river.

A useful statutory definition of what is a public road is to be found in the Road Traffic Act 1961 which states that a public road is a road, the responsibility for the maintenance of which lies with a road authority. The definition of a road pursuant to the Act includes: "any bridge, pipe, arch, gully, footway, pavement, fences, railings or wall forming part thereof..."[12]

6.   Obstruction of the Highway

Common Law

It was held that marching at the head of a band into a public square and there addressing a crowd constituted an obstruction of the highway.[13] A court may disregard insignificant obstructions, or ones which are temporary in character or those so small as not to impede traffic.[14]

---

[8] 2 Smith Leading Cases, 11th ed.,164.

[9] *Rangley v. Midland Railway Company* L.R.3 C.H. 306, *per* Lord Cairns.

[10] *Fisher v. Prowse* 2 Best & Smith Reports, Vol. 6, 10th ed., 1862 at 770; and see also *North London Railway Company v. Vestry of Saint Mary Islington* 21 W.R. 226.

[11] *Att. Gen. (Cork CC) v. Perry* [1904] 1 I.R. 247.

[12] Road Traffic Act 1961, s.3.

[13] *Homer v. Cadman* (1886) 16 Cox 51.

[14] *A.G. v. Mayo County Council* [1902] 1 I.R. and see *R. v. Bartholomew* [1908] 1 K.B. 554.

Statute Law

The Criminal Justice (Public Order) Act 1994, section 9 states that:

"Any person who, without lawful authority or reasonable excuse, wilfully prevents or interrupts the free passage of any person or vehicle shall be liable on summary conviction to a fine not exceeding £200..."

This may be difficult to prove because in some instances obstruction may be lawful depending on circumstances and duration. Statute law may also confer a right to obstruct a road where a road authority is carrying out repairs or it may be necessary for the police to obstruct the road in the exercise of their lawful powers.

An honest and reasonable belief in the right to cause the obstruction would seem to amount to a lawful excuse if it arose from a mistake of fact but not from a mistake of law, even if this mistake was induced by the police or a public authority.[15] It appears that in order to commit the offence of obstruction pursuant to section 9 of the Act, the obstruction must be done wilfully.

Definition of "Wilfully"

It has been stated that: "this definition amounts to nothing more than this: that he knows what he is doing, and intends to do what he is doing and is a free agent."[16] In *Eaton v. Cobb*, the driver of a car was held not to be wilful where he accidentally knocked a cyclist over.[17]

The question of obstruction of a public highway was discussed in the case of *Nagy v. Weston*. It was stated by Lord Parker that:

"It depends on all the circumstances including the length of time the obstruction continues, the place where it occurs, the purpose for which it is done and of course whether it does in fact cause an

---

[15] *Cambridgeshire and Isle of Ely County Council v. Rust* [1972] 2 Q.B. 426.

[16] *Young v. Hartson* 31 in *Re Young and Hartson's Contract*, 31 Ch. 1740, 174 per Bowen L.J.; see also dictum of Goddard L.C.J. in *Lomas v. Peek* [1947] 2 All E.R. 574-575. For discussion of the word "wilfully" see page 575.

[17] [1950] All E.R. 1016; 114 J.P. 271.

actual obstruction as opposed to a potential obstruction..."[18]

7.   The Right to Attend Public Meetings

It would appear that members of the public have a right to attend public meetings held in public places as of right, unless they commit a criminal offence or provoke a breach of the peace. Interjection or hecklings may not constitute a breach of the peace.[19]

Apart from members of the public having the right to attend public meetings, it follows that the press have the same right and are subject to the same legal obligations. But if a public meeting is held on private premises, the members of the public and the press may attend only if they comply with the regulations specified by the organisers and pay any fee required.

A member of the public or the press may be requested to leave such a meeting at the behest of the organisers at any time during the proceedings. The preservation of order in regard to such meetings lies within the powers of the organisers. However, the organisers may call in the Gardaí if a breach of the peace occurs and may arrest members who are suspected of such offences.

In *R. v. Howell* it was held that:

> "...there is a power of arrest for a breach of the peace where (1) a breach of the peace is committed in the presence of the person making the arrest or (2) the arrestor reasonably believes such a breach will be committed in the immediate future by the person arrested although he has not yet committed any breach, or (3) where a breach has been committed and it is reasonably believed that the renewal of it is threatened...[20]

---

[18] [1965] 1 W.L.R. 280 and 1 All E.R. 1965 at 80, *per* Parker C.J.

[19] See *Wooding v. Oxyley* Vol. 9 C.A.R. & P. (1835) 1 at 13.

[20] *R v. Howell* [1981] 3 All E.R. 388, *per* Watkins L.

8. Breach of the Peace

What constitutes a breach of the peace has been defined:

"...breach of the peace occurs when an act has been done or threatened to be done which either actually harms a person, or in his presence, his property, or is likely to cause such harm or which puts someone in fear of such harm being done or a person is in fear of being so harmed through an assault, an affray, a riot, an unlawful assembly or other disturbance. It is for this breach of the peace when done in his presence or the reasonable apprehension of it taking place that a constable or anyone else may arrest a person without warrant."[21]

At common law the Gardaí may not interfere with meetings held in private premises unless a breach of the peace has been, or is being, committed or where they have reasonable grounds for believing that a breach of the peace is likely to be committed.[22] However, the above must be considered in the context of the Criminal Justice (Public Order) Act 1994 which encompasses certain public order offences committed on private premises.

Section 15 of the 1994 Act abolished the common law offence of riot and unlawful assembly. There is now an offence of violent disorder. If the Gardaí decide to break up a meeting which may be unlawful or result in public disorder. The amount of force the Gardaí may use in breaking up a meeting must be reasonable, having regard to what has occurred.

In *Lynch v. Fitzgerald (No. 2)*[23] Hanna J. approved the dictum of Bowen L.J. from the Report of the Select Committee on the Fetherstone Riot 1893:

"By the Law of this Country everyone is bound to aid in the suppression of riotous assemblages, the degree of force however which may be used in their suppression depends on the nature of each riot for the force used must always be moderate and proportioned to the circumstances of the case and the end to be attained..."

Hanna J. made the following observations:

---

[21] *R v. Howell*, ibid., *per* Watkins L.J.
[22] *Thomas v. Sakins* [1935] 2 K.B. 249; see also 30 Cox 265.
[23] [1938] I.R. 382.
[24] *ibid.* at 382

"It is an invariable rule that the degree of force to be used must always be moderate and proportioned to the circumstances of the case and the end to be obtained, hence it is that arms...must be used with the greatest of care and the greatest pains must be exercised to avoid the infliction of fatal injuries...a gun should never be used or used with any specified degree of force if there is any doubt as to its necessity."[24]

9. Picketing

If a picket constitutes the offence of watching and besetting it is unlawful under the Conspiracy and Protection of Property Act 1875[25] unless the watching and besetting can be justified as part of a trade dispute.[26] In *Hubbard v. Pitt* the defendants, a local pressure group, picketed the offices of a firm of estate agents by standing in a line along the public footpath, holding placards and distributing leaflets; there was a space on either side of the picket line for individual members of the public to pass. An injunction was granted on the basis that this was not an industrial dispute. This was upheld in the Court of Appeal on the basis of it being a private nuisance. Denning L.J., dissenting, stated that:

"the right to picket is not confined to industrial disputes and is lawful so long as it is done merely to obtain or communicate information or peacefully persuade, the right to demonstrate and protest were rights which were in the public interest that individuals should possess and exercise without impediment so long as no wrongful act is done".[27]

---

[25] See the Conspiracy and Protection of Property Act 1875 s.7 in which it states that: "It is a criminal offence for a person wrongfully and without legal authority to watch and beset the house or other place where another person resides or works or carries on business or happens to be, or the approach to such house or place with a view to compel such other person to abstain from doing or to do any act which such other person has a legal right to do or abstain from doing..." Note this is a scheduled offence under s.36 of the Offences against the State Act 1939. The provisions contained in the Trade Dispute Act 1906 in relation to conspiracy and combination have been re-enacted without any amendments to the Industrial Relations Act 1990, s.10.

[26] The relevant statutory provisions in relation to trade disputes in general are now contained in the Industrial Relations Act 1990 as the Trade Dispute Act 1906 is fully repealed.

[27] [1975] 3 All E.R.

This line of thought was followed in *Hirst v. Chief Constable of West Yorkshire Police* where Otton J. stated that:

"...the right to demonstrate and protest on matters of public concern are rights which are in the public interest that individuals should possess and exercise without impediment as long as no wrongful act is done and there is no obstruction to traffic..."[28]

The question of the right to picket in furtherance of a trade dispute, pursuant to the Trade Disputes Act 1906 (now repealed and substantially re-enacted in the Industrial Relations Act 1990) was examined in *Dunne v. Fitzpatrick* in which Budd J. set the following principles:

"The existence of a Trade Dispute involves the right to picket but it still remains to be decided whether or not a particular form of picketing adopted by the defendants was justified under the provisions of the Act. This entitles a person acting of himself or of a trade union in furtherance of a trade dispute to attend at or near a place where a person works or carries on business if they so attend merely for the purpose of peacefully obtaining or communicating information or of peacefully persuading any person to work or abstain from work."[29]

However, it was held in *Goulding Chemicals v. Bolger* that picketing was not lawful if it was designed to intimidate, having regard to number of particpants, their manner and language.[30] It appears that placards disseminating a falsehood do not constitute peaceful communication.[31] In deciding if a picket is unlawful it is necessary to look at the numbers involved and the language used.[32]

---

[28] [1986] 151 J.P. 25.
[29] [1958] I.R. 29 at 43.
[30] Unreported, High Court, Budd J., May 26, 1977.
[31] *Ryan v. Cook and Quinn*, [1938] I.R. 512.
[32] *Education Company of Ireland v. Kennedy*, [1968] I.R. 69

In order to be afforded statutory immunity from civil proceedings it is necessary that the statutory provisions of the Industrial Relations Act 1990 be satisfied. However, the Supreme Court recently appeared to take the view that, in a case where the statutory procedures were not fully complied with, this did not deprive the defendant from availing of the statutory immunity provided under the 1990 Act.[33]

---

[33] *SIPTU v. Nolan Transport (Oaklands) Limited*, The *Irish Times,* Supreme Court, May 16, 1998.

2. The Criminal Justice (Public Order) Act 1994

The law of meetings in Ireland has been affected by the Criminal Justice (Public Order) Act 1994. This Act abolished many of the offences regarding public order at common law and replaced them with a number of new statutory public order offences. The Act also provides the Garda Síochána at Part III of the Act with powers to control crowds and deal with access by persons to certain events.

This chapter will deal with the offences under the Act which relate specifically to the law of meetings.

1. Threatening, Abusive or Insulting Behaviour in a Public Place

This matter is dealt with in section 6(1) of the Act which states:

"It shall be an offence for any person in a public place to use or engage in any threatening abusive or insulting words or behaviour with intent to provoke a breach of the peace or being reckless as to whether a breach of the peace may be occasioned."

In order to secure a conviction under this section, it is necessary that the offence be committed in a public place. It also follows that the words or behaviour must be used with an intention to provoke a breach of the peace.

It would appear that mere heckling of speakers at a public meeting does not fall within the definition of what constitutes a breach of the peace. In *Wooding v. Oxley* it was held that mere proof of annoyance and disturbance such as crying "hear, hear", asking the speaker petty questions and making observations on the speaker's statement would not constitute a breach of the peace.[1]

---

[1] *Wooding v. Oxyley* [1835] 9 CAR & PI; see also *Russell on Crime* (12th ed.), p.227 on King (Williams) Case 1588 4 Co. Inst. 181.

However, words tending to a breach of the peace may constitute an offence if one man challenges another by words.[2] But it would be necessary to prove that the words used were intended to provoke the person to whom they were addressed to give challenge.[3]

2. Distribution or display in public place of material which is threatening, abusive, insulting or obscene

Section 7(1) of the Act provides that:

> "It shall be an offence for any person in a public place to distribute or display any writing, sign or visible representation which is threatening, abusive, insulting or obscene with intent to provoke a breach of the peace or being reckless as to whether a breach of the peace may occasioned..."

This offence is committed only if the material in question is displayed or distributed in a public place. It would, therefore, appear that no offence is committed if the material in question is displayed on private premises, even if seen by members of the public. The *mens rea* (guilty mind) of this crime is the intent to provoke a breach of the peace or being reckless as to whether a breach of the peace may be occasioned.

It is arguable that the innocent dissemination of information may not fall within this definition. However, what may be regarded as threatening, abusive, insulting or obscene to one member of the public may not affect another in a similar manner. This test could be viewed as being subjective. This section has been invoked against certain groups involved in street campaigning, for instance, on the pro-life issue.

3. Riot

Section 14(1) provides that:

> "(a) where   12   or   more   persons   who   are   present
>   together   at   any   place   (whether   the   place   is   a   public

---

[2] *R. v. Langley (1794)* 6 Mod 125.
[3] *Russell on Crime* (10th ed.) Stevens & Co., London, 1950. p.265.

place or a private place or both) use or threaten to use
unlawful violence for a common purpose, and
(b) the conduct of those persons, taken together, in such
place as would cause a person of reasonable firmness
present at that place, to fear for his or another person's
safety

then, each of the persons using unlawful violence for the common
purpose shall be guilty of the offence of riot."

This offence can be committed in a public or private place or in both.[4] It
is immaterial whether or not the 12 or more persons use or threaten to use
unlawful violence simultaneously at any place.[5] The common purpose
may be inferred from conduct.[6]

It appears from this section that where 12 or more persons use or
threaten to use unlawful violence, if only one of that group is apprehended and is proved to have used or have intended to use or threaten to use
unlawful violence, the remaining members of the group are guilty of riot
even though they were not apprehended or proved to have the necessary
mens rea. In order to secure a conviction under this section, it is not necessary to prove that personal violence was actually committed.[7] No person of reasonable firmness need actually be or be likely to be present at
the place.[8]

4. Violent Disorder

Section 15(1) provides that where:

"(a) three or more persons who are present together at any place
(whether that place is a public place or private place or both) use
or threaten to use unlawful violence, and
(b) the conduct of those persons, taken together, is such as would
cause a person of reasonable firmness, present at that place, to

---

[4] Criminal Justice (Public Order) Act 1994, s.14(1)(a).

[5] *ibid.*, s.14(2)(a) and (b).

[6] *ibid.*, s.14(2)(b).

[7] *Clifford v. Brandon* 2 Camps, *per* Mansfield J.

[8] The 1994 Act, above, n.4, s.14(2)(c).

fear for his or another person's safety

then, each of the person's using or threatening to use unlawful violence shall be guilty of the offence of violent disorder."

This offence may be committed in a public or private place.[9] There must be three or more persons present together.[10] It is similar to the offence of riot, in that it is immaterial whether or not those three or more persons use or threaten to use violence simultaneously.[11] It also follows that no person of reasonable firmness need be present at the scene.[12] The *mens rea* of this crime is that a person shall not be convicted of the offence of violent disorder unless the person intends to use or threatens to use violence or is aware that his conduct may be violent or threaten violence.[13] This provision abolished the common law offence of rout and unlawful assembly.[14]

5. Affray

Section 16(1) provides that where:

"(a) two or more persons at any place (whether the place is a public place or a private place or both) use or threaten to use violence towards each other, and
(b) the violence so used or threatened by one of these persons is unlawful, and
(c) the conduct of those persons, taken together, is such as would cause a person of reasonable firmness, present at that place, to fear for his or another person's safety

then each person who uses or threatens to use unlawful violence shall be guilty of the offence of affray."

---

[9] s.15(1)(a).
[10] *ibid.*
[11] s.15(2)(a).
[12] s.15(2)(b).
[13] s.15(3).
[14] s.15(6).

The offence may be committed in a public or private place.[15] The threat cannot be made by words alone.[16] It is not necessary that a person of reasonable firmness be present at the scene.[17]

A person shall not be convicted of the offence of affray unless the person intends to use, or threatens to use, violence or is aware that his conduct may be violent or threaten violence.[18] It would appear that although at least two persons are required, under the Act, to constitute an affray, one person can be convicted of the offence.[19] Where two or more persons use or threaten the unlawful violence, the conduct of all of them must be considered. One English commentator has stated that: "an affray can exist without actual violence if persons arm themselves with dangerous and unusual weapons in such a manner which will naturally cause terror to the people".[20]

The Gardaí have extensive powers of arrest where they find persons committing offences under the Act or are of the opinion that an offence has been committed. The Gardaí may also demand the name and address of any person who they suspect or find committing an offence and if that person refuses to give their name and address, or gives a false or misleading one, they may be arrested without warrant and shall also be guilty of an offence.[21]

6. Crowd Control at Public Events

Section 20 of the Act provides the Gardaí with statutory authority to deal with crowd control at public events. These provisions are reflective of the recommendations of the Hamilton Committee on Public Safety and Crowd Control.[22]

This section enables a member of the Garda Síochána, not below the

---

[15] s.10(a).

[16] s.16(2)(a).

[17] s.16(2)(b).

[18] s.16(3).

[19] *D.P.P v. Button* [1965] 3 All E.R. 587.

[20] *Russell on Crime* (10th ed.), p.265.

[21] s.24(1)-(4). This section applies under the Act to offences committed under ss. 4, 6–8, 11, 13–19.

[22] Committee on Public Safety and Crowd Control, Stationery Office, Dublin, February 1990.

rank of Superintendent, for the purpose of safety or preservation of order, to restrict the access of persons to events; it provides that the Gardaí may erect barriers, for a distance not greater than one mile from the venue in question and allows a Garda to divert people to the place of access where they possess a ticket and prohibit them from going into the area if they have no ticket. It also allows the Gardaí to confiscate intoxicating liquor or offensive articles. However, these provisions should not be used to hinder persons going to their workplace or homes. A person failing to comply with an order of the Garda Síochána shall be liable, on summary conviction, to a fine of £500.

If a member of the Garda Síochána suspects that a person has in his or her possession any intoxicating liquor, disposable container, or any article which could cause injury, he or she can refuse that person permission to proceed any further and he or she may cause that person to be searched. If persons are found to be in possession of these items, they may be ordered to leave in an orderly manner. If a person fails to so leave, he or she may be liable, on summary conviction, to a fine of £500.[22]

---

[23] ss. 20-22.

Part Two: Meetings and Procedures

3. Notice

A private meeting of a non-constituted body can dispense with all formalities in regard to the holding of a meeting if the organisers so desire, unless the meeting is of a nature as would affect the rights of or impose obligations on any person. The main concern for organisers of such a meeting is that they do not commit a breach of the peace or leave themselves open to a civil action, should they cause a disturbance. Constituted bodies are those organisations which have specific rules which govern their activities, *e.g.* clubs, societies, limited companies, etc.

These meetings may and invariably do affect rights and impose obligations and therefore it is necessary that such meetings observe proper procedure and are properly constituted. A constituted body may have written rules to govern the holding of meetings. It would also appear to follow that if there are no rules in place, then the principles of common law and natural and constitutional justice, if any, will be applicable.[1]

1. Convening Meetings and Notice

A meeting is usually convened by way of notice, subject to the regulations of a constituted body which may provide otherwise. Notice should be given to all those who are entitled to attend the meeting.[2]

Valid notice of a meeting should observe a number of essential elements. The responsibility for ensuring valid notice is given lies with the secretary, where one has been appointed, or with the organisers.

1. Valid notice should inform those entitled to attend a meeting, of the date, time and place of the meeting.

2. It should set out the reason and purpose of the meeting. It should comply with any statutory obligations that are relevant.

---

[1] See Chap. 14 on meetings and natural justice.
[2] *R. v. Shrewsbury* 1735 Cases Lee Temp Hardwicke 147 and *Re Homer District Consolidated Goldmines, ex p. Smith*, 39 Ch. & D. 546.

3.   It should be clearly set out and unambiguous.

4.   Notice of the meeting must be given to all those entitled to attend.

5.   It should conform with the prescribed rules or standing orders, if any, of the organisation or body.

6.   It should conform with the basic principles of natural justice as relevant.[3]

Section 134 (a) of the Companies Act 1963 states that: "notice of the meeting of a company shall be served on every member of the company in the manner in which notices are required to be served by Table A..."

If a person has a duty to attend a meeting, it also follows that he or she must receive notice of such a meeting. This matter was discussed in the case of *Young v. Ladies Imperial Club*.[4] In this case a member of a ladies club was expelled by the committee for behaviour inconsistent with the rules of the club. An enquiry revealed that notice of the committee meeting had not been sent to a committee member who had previously stated that she could not attend meetings and the evidence revealed that she had never in fact done so. It was held on appeal that failure to give notice according to the rules invalidated the proceedings of the meeting.

Certain persons have statutory rights to receive notice of a meeting, *e.g.* the auditor of a company under section 163(4) of the Companies Act 1963. If a person is beyond summoning distance, or suffers from a severe illness and cannot be moved, then this may be sufficient reason for not summoning him or her.[5] If a member is unable to attend but has the right to appoint a proxy to vote in his absence and appoints such a proxy the principles stated above have no application.[6] In *Warden v. Hotchkiss Limited*, a company pursuant to its articles of association was required to

---

[3] See Chap. 14, p.50.

[4] [1920] 2 K.B. 523.

[5] While this is common law principle, many organisations are subject to statutory provisions regarding notice and one should note also the basic principles of natural and constitutional justice.

[6] *Re Union Hill Silver Company* [1870] 22 L.T. 400.

give seven days' notice to its members, although if any member did not receive notice, this would not invalidate proceedings at any general meeting. Notice was served on every member entitled to vote, but there were five who had addresses in South Africa, all of whom agreed with the resolution altering the memorandum and articles of association. Uthwatt J., having considered the articles of the company, held that the meeting was not properly convened and that the resolution in question was invalid.[7]

The rules of a body may contain provisions regarding the accidental omission to give notice. An example of this can be found in the case of a company whose articles are based on Table A of the Companies Act 1963, where it is provided for by Article 52 of the Table: "that the accidental omission to give notice of a meeting to any person entitled to receive such notice shall not invalidate the proceedings in question..."

It was held in *Re The West Canadian Collieries* that an accidental omission to give notice of a meeting would not invalidate proceedings. The company's registrar failed to give notice of the meeting to nine of the shareholders because addressograph plates had been mislaid. This failure to give notice was excused by the court and the meeting which was held was deemed valid. However, a deliberate failure to give notice of a meeting will invalidate the meeting.[8]

Lack of proper notice may be waived if all of those entitled to such notice are present at the meeting and none object.[9] The notice issued must be adequate. In *Roper v. Ward*, an Irish case, it was held that notice convening a meeting concerning resolutions proposing to give shares, in the distribution of surplus assets, to persons who were not full members or associate members, was defective. It did not give adequate notice of the general nature of the special business.[10]

Where notice is issued it must be adequate to provide reasonable time for members to attend.[11] The secretary of a company may issue notice of a meeting, subject to the authority of the board of directors. However, if the secretary issues the notice without proper authority, it may be subsequently ratified by the convening authority before the meeting takes place.[12]

---

[7] [1945] 1 All E.R. 268; see also *Re Anglo International Bank Limited* [1943] 1 Ch. 233.

[8] *Musselwhite v. Musselwhite (C.H.)& Son Ltd.* [1962] 2 Ch. 964.

[9] *Oxted Motor Company* [1921] 3 K.B. 32.

[10] [1981] I.L.R.M. 408.

[11] *Re Homer District Consolidated Goldmines, ex p. Smith*, above, n.2.

[12] *Hooper v. Kerr Stuart* [1900] 83 L.T. 729.

Notice of a meeting should contain details referring generally to such matters as the date, time and place of the meeting. It should specify the type of meeting and must include special business.[13] The notice should also distinguish between ordinary and special business and must be of such a nature as not to mislead.[14]

In assessing the contents of the notice the courts will apply the following test: "what does it convey to ordinary minds?"[15]

It would appear that it is not a general requirement that notice be given of an adjourned meeting, if all members were present when the adjournment occurred. But notice must be given of an adjournment *sine die* or if new business will be discussed. If the notice to convene a meeting has not yet issued, the board of directors may meet and rescind their decision to call such a meeting.[16] However, if the notice has been issued the meeting must be held, and may then, subject to agreement, be adjourned.[17] The notice regarding this adjournment must be circulated to all members. An exception to this would be if the notice was given at the meeting out of which the adjournment occurred, then this would be deemed adequate.[18]

A person who is present and who votes at a meeting will not be entitled to challenge its validity.[19] The method of issuing a notice may be specified in the rules of an organisation. In the case of a company limited by shares, which has been incorporated pursuant Table A of the first schedule of the Companies Act 1963, the mode of notice is clearly set out.[20] If the articles of association of a company specify that the service of notice must be by post, this means ordinary Irish post.[21]

If the rules specify a method of service that must be strictly adhered to. If the regulations do not provide the day on which notice is served or deemed to be served, in accordance with the meaning of the

---

[13] See *Roper v. Ward*, above, n.10.

[14] *Kaye v. Croydon Tramways* [1898] 1 Ch. 358; see also *Jackson v. Munster Bank* [1884–1885] L.R. 118

[15] See *Henderson v. Bank of Australasia* [1890] 45 Ch. D. 330.

[16] This occurs in the postponing of a meeting as distinct from an adjournment.

[17] *Smith v. Paringa Mines* [1906] 2 Ch. 193.

[18] *Kerr v. Wilkie* [1860] I.L.T. 501.

[19] *British Sugar Refining Co.* [1857] 3 K & J 408.

[20] Table A, art. 51, Companies Act 1963, deals generally with the notices required for a company meeting but must be read in conjunction with ss. 133 and 141.

[21] *Re Union Hill Silver Company*, above, n. 6.

word "service", an interpretation may have to be ascertained from the Interpretation Act 1937.[22] If the rules of an organisation contain no such regulations, then any reasonable and fair method will do.

Notice is presumed to mean "clear notice" exclusive both of the day on which it is served and the day of the meeting.[23]

In regard to meetings generally, it is essential that all regulations of a constituted body should be examined in a prudent manner so as to find out if any provisions exist concerning the service of notice.

---

[22] Where a period of time is expressed to begin on or be reckoned from a particular day, that day shall, unless the contrary intention appears, be deemed to be included in such period and where a period of time is so expressed to end or be reckoned to a particular day, that day unless the contrary intention appears shall be deemed to be included in such period; s.11(ii)(h) Interpretation Act 1937.

[23] *Re Neil M'Leod & Sons* [1967] S.L.T. 46.

4. The Agenda

An agenda means literally "things to be done". In the context of meetings it normally refers to the document which lists the items of business to be dealt with at a meeting. An agenda which is circulated among those entitled to attend a meeting informs such persons of the main purpose and business to be considered. In *Holland v. McGill*, Murphy J. stated the following in relation to an agenda : "There is no requirement to provide directors with an agenda of a meeting though in practice it may be desirable that it be done occasionally if not frequently and if supplied must be accurate..."[1]

The length and form of an agenda can vary according to the nature and requirements of the organisation. Many agendas take the form of a skeleton outline of the matters to be dealt with. A more detailed form of agenda may be composed, containing substantial information on the matters to be discussed, and may include proposed motions or resolutions to be put to the meeting.

Contents of an Agenda

The following matters are usually set out on an agenda paper:

1. It should have a heading indicating the place, date and time of a meeting.

2. The items of business should be set out in order, ideally by number according to the standing orders and rules, if any, of the meeting. The first items listed on the agenda will usually concern routine matters, such as approval of the minutes of the previous meeting and apologies from non-attenders. Special or non-routine matters, which may require more lengthy discussion, will be placed further down the list.

---

[1] Unreported, High Court, Murphy J. March 16, 1990.

3.   It should be noted that the only business which should be placed on an agenda is that which comes within the scope of the notice convening the meeting and is within the authority of the meeting to discuss and consider.

4.   All relevant items of business to be discussed should be listed with a note explaining the business. It is normally the duty of the secretary to ensure that notice of a meeting is circulated and that an agenda be compiled. The secretary should liase and consult with the chairman and any other officers or committee members that may wish to have business included in the agenda.

5.   If persons will be attending to address, advise or consult the meeting this should be stated, if possible, with the order of business on the agenda paper.

6.   An agenda will normally contain a heading "Any Other Business" to facilitate the discussion of business which may not be routine but is not so important that advance notice needs to be given. However, sometimes this heading may be used by persons attending the meeting as a tactic to bring forward business that properly should have been flagged as an item of business on the agenda paper. If this is attempted, it is normally within the discretion of the chairperson to prevent any decisions being taken on a significant matter, until the next meeting, for example.

      However, if a matter is urgent and requires consideration prior to the next meeting the chairperson may allow discussion and if necessary a vote or decision by whatever method necessary.[2]

7.   The agenda should not be circulated until it has been approved whether informally by the chairperson or in the case of a company incorporated under the Companies Acts by resolution of the board of directors.

The general order of business on an agenda paper can vary. However, a

---

[2] It may require the suspension of standing orders in the manner prescribed by the rules of the body in question.

standard agenda for a small non-company meeting will be laid as follows:

1. Apologies for absence (this may not be practical for larger meetings).

2. The nomination and proposal of new members, as relevant to the type of meeting.

3. The minutes of the last meeting are read and approved by the chairperson.

4. Any correspondence received by the organisation or body since the last meeting.

5. Reports from any officers or other persons to be considered by the meeting.

At this stage in the order of business the meeting may consider suspending standing orders if such exist to allow discussion of matters otherwise prohibited by standing orders where for example there is a requirement for a specific quorum.

6. Items of business of a non-routine nature.

7. Any other business.

The chairperson may wish to take items of business in a different sequence and he should advise the meeting of his reasons for doing so. If there is no consensus, then this matter may have to be debated and a decision, by way of motion, for example, may have to be taken in relation to the order of business.

A skeleton agenda for a company limited by shares could read as follows:

XY LIMITED

AGENDA

1.   Directors' report and accounts.

2.   Auditors' Report.

3.   Dividend.

4.   Election of Directors.

5.   Remuneration of Auditor.

The agenda paper no longer has any importance after the conclusion of business of the meeting except that the secretary may wish to retain a copy to assist in drafting the minutes.

5. The Chairperson and Secretary

A chairperson (traditionally "chairman") is the person who regulates the proceedings of a meeting. If there are no regulations providing for appointment of a chairperson, one can be appointed by those in attendance at the meeting. This may be done by consensus among those present, or if nominations are called for, by a vote, whether by a show of hands or secret ballot. This process is most likely to occur when a new body or organisation is being set up.

If the organisation has regulations which set out what is to happen at a meeting in the absence of a chairperson (or vice/deputy chairperson), these will prevail in terms of the procedure to appoint a chairperson for that meeting.

The chairperson, once elected or appointed by whatever rules applicable to that organisation, has a duty to ensure that the business of the meeting is conducted in a proper manner.

There are a number of clearly recognised functions of a chairperson which illustrate his authority in controlling a meeting. These include:

1.   to maintain order and prevent unwarranted disruption;

2.   to ensure the meeting is conducted in accordance with law and within the applicable regulations, rules and/or standing orders of the organisation; and

3.   to further ensure that the principles of due process and natural justice are observed giving all those entitled to attend an opportunity to be heard in so far as is practicable and conducive to the orderly running of the meeting.

The chairperson will also have a responsibility to ensure that the proceedings and decisions of the meeting are formally recorded by a secretary, or someone in a similar capacity.

The rulings of the chairperson on points of order raised are deemed, prima facie, to be correct.[1] The chairperson normally has a casting vote where there is an equality or deadlock of votes. A statutory recognition of this solution where an equality of votes arises can be seen in the Companies Act 1963, Table A, Article 61.[2]

In *Byng v. London Life Association Limited* a company meeting was held in a small venue with overflow facilities to which a lot of members could not gain access. There was an audio-visual link between the overflow rooms and the floor of the meeting. However, the link was not functioning properly and some of the members in the overflow areas could not hear the chairman.

The meeting was adjourned until later that afternoon and moved to another venue. A shareholder of the company brought an action that that the chairman had not validly adjourned the first meeting and that the business of the afternoon meeting was conducted invalidly.

In the Court of Appeal, Nicholas Browne V.C. considered carefully the role of a chairperson in regard to his powers of adjournment and clearly stated that:

> "A chairman has no general right to adjourn a meeting of his own will and pleasure, there being no circumstances preventing the effective continuation of proceedings...It is clearly established that a Chairman has such powers where unruly conduct prevents the continuation of business. It is also established that when in an orderly meeting a poll is demanded the Chairman has power to suspend the meeting with a view to its continuance at a later date after the result of the poll is nown."

He further stated that there was a residual power in the Chairman to take such steps as would, in the ordinary usage of the word, amount to an adjournment. Where there is a meeting at which the view of the majority cannot be validly ascertained, the Chairman has a residual common law power to adjourn so as to give all persons entitled a reasonable opportu-

---

[1] *John v. Rees* [1970] Ch. 345.

[2] It states: "Where there is an equality of votes, whether on a show of hands or on a poll, the chairman of the meeting at which the show of hands takes place, or at which the poll is demanded, shall be entitled to a second or casting vote."

nity of voting. But there must be very special circumstances to justify a decision to adjourn.[3]

The chairperson may exercise a casting vote given to him.[4] A person cannot complain, in the absence of any proof of what Lord Shaw in the case of *Loch v. John Blackwood Limited* referred to as lack of probity in the conduct of the company's affairs.[5]

The chairperson may adjourn, on his own authority, in order to allow the business of a meeting which could include taking a valid poll. In *R v. D'Oyly* it was stated that, irrespective of the inconvenience that might arise if the majority of parishioners could determine the point of adjournment, the person who presides at the meeting is the proper individual to decide this. Lord Denman went on to say that: "it devolves both to preserve order in a meeting and to regulate the proceedings so as to give all persons entitled a reasonable opportunity of voting."

His Lordship concluded that: "He has to do acts necessary for these purposes on his own responsibility and subject to being called upon to answer for his conduct if he has done anything improperly."[6] The chairperson will declare the results of any election.

1. The Secretary

The secretary has an overall responsibility for the smooth running of the body or organisation and more particularly for ensuring that its meetings are properly organised. A secretary must draft and issue notices and draw up the agenda. He advises the chairperson on procedural aspects of the meeting and, in this regard, communicates with the appropriate legal officers. They prepare any proxy notices/draft minutes and ensure that they are signed by the chairman.

There are no professional qualifications required of a secretary either generally or pursuant to the Companies Acts. However, in the case of a public limited company, for example, the directors must ensure that a secretary has the appropriate experience and knowledge to carry out his

---

[3] *Byng v. London Life Association Limited* [1990] Ch. 170.

[4] *Re Expanded Plugs* [1966] 1 All E.R. 877.

[5] [1924] 2 A.C. 783.

[6] (1840) 12 A.& E. 139 at 159; See also *John v. Rees* [1969] 2 All E.R. 877.

or her duties and functions.[7]

2.   Points of Order

A point of order is a statement made to enable a member to interrupt a meeting. This would occur where there is a procedural defect regarding the meeting in question. An example would be where there is a failure to maintain a quorum and the chairperson is unaware of this. The chairperson's rule on a point of order is final.

---

[7] The statutory duties of a company secretary are set out in section 175 of the Companies Act 1963.

6. Minutes

Minutes are the formal written record of the business transacted at a meeting.

The contents of minutes will usually include a heading setting out:

1.   the name of the body or organisation which held the meeting;

2.   the type of meeting, whether a residents' association meeting, or an annual general Meeting pursuant to the Companies Acts.

3.   the place, date and time of the meeting.

The contents will normally list those entitled to be present and may also record apologies for non-attendance. This would be the practice for board meetings or smaller gatherings or assemblies. For larger meetings the numbers present may be all that is recorded in the minutes.

The minutes should contain records of decisions taken and resolutions passed.

Some minutes will record the names of proposers and seconders of resolutions passed. In large meetings this may not be practicable.

The minutes are often numbered per item of business for accuracy and ease of reference.

The chairperson normally signs the minutes when prepared and drafted at the commencement of the following meeting. The chairperson usually signs the minutes after they have been read to the subsequent meeting and verified by him for their accuracy. There is usually a resolution passed by the subsequent meeting approving the adoption of the minutes.

1. Essentials of Minutes

Minutes should be:

1.   authentic;
2.   accurate;
3.   concise yet complete; and
4.   clear and unambiguous.

The minutes should state the day, date, time and place of the meeting. The minutes should be in sufficient detail, giving the full text of resolutions, for example. However, unlike a report, it would be unnecessary to record debates and discussions in detail prior to the passing of a resolution.

Minutes are usually in printed form; however, there is no rule prohibiting the drafting of minutes in hand-written form. Minutes can be loose leaf. They should reflect the order of business. Confidentiality and security must be provided for the keeping of minutes.

The minutes of a meeting are not exclusive evidence of what takes place. An unrecorded resolution may be proved *aliunde* (elsewhere).[1]

Section 146 of the Companies Act 1963 provides that the minutes of a company meeting should be available for inspection for two hours each day to any member. It also provides that a member may, on request, be facilitated in making copies of minutes, for a fee.

Section 4(1) of the Companies Act 1977 allows for the use of non-legible computer recording of certain company matters including company meetings, provided that they can be reproduced in legible form.

---

[1] *Knight's case* [1807] 2 Ch. 321; and also *Re Fireproof Doors* (1916) 2 Ch. 142.

7. Quorum

The word "quorum" has been defined in the Oxford English Dictionary as: "the minimum number of people that must be present to constitute a valid meeting". A meeting ordinarily requires the presence of at least two members who are entitled to take part in the proceedings although, in effect there is no general rule specified as to what should constitute a quorum of a constituted body.

There are statutory provisions, which deal with the question of quorums in relation to certain bodies. A company registered under the Companies Act 1963 requires at least two members to constitute a valid meeting.[1]

In the case of a private company, the quorum shall consist of at least two members and in the case of other companies, three members present in person shall be a quorum. There are also provisions regarding quorums in the area of local government.[2]

This provision was referred to in *Sharpe v. Dawes*: one member of a company attended a company meeting at which the secretary of the company was also present. This member held proxies for other absent members. This meeting was held to be invalid as the meeting was not properly constituted.[3]

This issue was also considered in *Re London Flats*, in which two members were, in the circumstances, the only persons entitled to attend and vote at company meetings. A general meeting had been convened of which notice had been given to appoint a liquidator. One member declared himself as chairperson though the other member objected. The first member then invited the other member to propose the resolution set out in the notice which he read out in full. He then stated that he proposed an amendment to the resolution proposing himself as liquidator. However, the other party had left the room before he did make the proposal. The amendment was put to a vote and there was one vote in favour and none against. The first member declared the amendment carried. It was held that the member's proposed appointment of himself as liquida-

[1] See Companies Act 1963, s.134.
[2] See Chap. 16, concerning quorums and public bodies.
[3] (1876) 2 Q.B.D. 29.

tor was null because at the moment when he was proposing himself, the other member had left the meeting and from that time there was only one member present and, therefore, no meeting. It followed, therefore, that a single shareholder could not as a general rule constitute a general meeting.[4]

If a body or organisation has no legal provisions or regulations providing for a rule that two members or persons shall constitute a quorum, then it would appear to follow that one person may constitute a quorum (though in practice this may create difficulty from an administrative point of view). The preferred view is that the greater number of those entitled to attend should be present at a meeting. This would seem to be, in the absence of statute or internal regulations in terms of the body itself, a simple majority.[5]

However, it is rare now that any body or organisation—even more so a company with articles of association incorporated pursuant to the Companies Acts – meeting formally would not have standing orders or regulations to cover the issue of a quorum at any meeting.

1.   Ascertaining a Quorum

At a shareholders' meeting where the articles of association allow for voting by proxy, where there is no poll, the chairman, in ascertaining the number of votes given, must count the votes of each person who has appointed a proxy not according to the number of shares held by him but as one.[6] This means that one counts the members present in person and also the votes of those present appointed by proxy.

---

[4] [1969] 1 W.L.R. 711, [1969] 2 All E.R. 744. However, see European Communities (Single Member Private Limited Companies) S.I. 275 1994, for an exception to s.134 (c). Also note that under s.135 (1) of the Companies Act 1963 the court may in certain circumstances order that a meeting be called and direct that one member of a company present in person or by proxy shall be deemed to constitute a quorum. In *Angelis v. Algemene Bank Nederland (Ireland) Ltd*, unreported, High Court, Kenny J., July 4, 1974 it was stated that a court would not easily make such an order. See also *Harman & another v. BML Group Limited*, [1994] 2 B.C.L.C. 674. The Minister for Enterprise can, pursuant to s.131(3) of the Companies Act 1963, make an order that a general meeting be convened and designate that one person present in person or by proxy shall constitute the necessary quorum.

[5] See *McColl v. Horne and Young* (1886) 6 N.Z.L.R. 590 and see also European Communities (Single Member Private Limited Companies) Regulations 1994.

[6] [1893] 1 Ch. 603.

2. Constituting a Quorum

The person constituting the quorum in question must attend with the intention of convening a meeting. In *Barron v. Potter*, two directors were unable to agree as to the conduct of the business of the company and they refused to see each other at board meetings. Barron requisitioned a general meeting in order to approve a resolution to remove Potter from the board and also to appoint additional directors. The day before the general meeting Potter met Barron coming off the train at Paddington Station and proposed that a certain person be elected a director of the company. Barron replied that he had nothing to say and continued walking on. Potter, as chairman of the company, gave his casting vote and declared the resolution carried. Subsequently, Potter visited Barron in his office prior to the general meeting and proposed the appointment of certain additional directors. Barron refused to make a comment on the matter. Potter then exercised his casting vote and declared them elected. It was held that this meeting was invalid.[7]

At any company meeting the personal representatives of a deceased shareholder can not, prior to their registration as members of the company, make up a quorum at a meeting of the company.[8]

The quorum, if required, must be maintained throughout the meeting at which a decision may be arrived at. It follows that if the members of a quorum withdraw from the meeting prior to the decision being arrived at, it may cause the meeting and the decision to be invalid.[9]

3. Maintaining a Quorum

If a meeting commences with the requisite quorum and prior to a decision being arrived at a number of members leave, any vote which is taken may be deemed invalid.[10]

---

[7] [1914] 1 Ch. 895.

[8] *Arulchelvan v. Wright*, unreported, High Court, Carroll J., February 2, 1995.

[9] *Re London Flats*, above, n.4.

[10] *ibid.*

4.   Disinterested Quorum

A failure to maintain a quorum may occur in a situation where the meeting commences with the number required to make up the quorum but some of those members are subsequently discovered to be disqualified, *e.g.* persons having a pecuniary interest in the matter under discussion at a local authority meeting.

Where the company's articles of association provide for a quorum of directors to deal with certain matters and if part of that quorum is composed of directors who have a personal interest in the matter under discussion, any resolution passed at such meeting will be invalid.[11]

---

[11] *North Eastern Insurance Company* [1919] 1 Ch. 198.

8. Motions and Amendments

A motion is a specific proposition put before a meeting for discussion, possibly resulting in a decision. The contents of a motion must be framed in positive terms. It must be clear, certain and unambiguous. A motion can be distinguished from a resolution; although similar in nature a resolution is more appropriate for company meetings.

There is no rule at common law that a motion must be seconded.[1] Any motion which is put before a meeting must be drafted in a manner that corresponds to the notice that convenes the meeting. Once a motion is before a meeting it can only be withdrawn with the consent of the meeting convened.[2] In the absence of specified rules on motions relevant to a meeting, a member proposing a motion may speak only once for the purpose of proposing the motion and can make further comment on the motion only if invited to do so by the chairperson. This may arise where clarification of some matter regarding the motion is necessary. The meeting may then resolve to accept the motion and so, in effect, it will become a decision of the meeting.

1. Types of Motion

1. Dilatory motions. This type of motion is used to delay the business. An example would be a constant stream of interruptions by way of points of order so that the business of the meeting is delayed.

2. That the meeting proceed to next business. If this motion is carried the meeting concludes the matter under discussion and proceeds to the next item of business.

3. Kangaroo motions. This describes where a meeting considers

---

[1] *Re Horbury Bridge Coal Company* [1879] 11 Ch. D. 109.
[2] *Choppington Collieries Limited v. Johnson* [1944] 1 All E.R. 762; see also the Companies Act 1963, s.141(1) regarding notice for special resolutions.

items of business on the agenda paper in a random manner.

4.   Guillotine motion. This occurs where a prescribed period of time is allotted to the matter under discussion and when the period has expired the meeting is prevented from having any further discussion on the matter.

5.   Letting the matter lie. This motion may occur where a report or other document is being discussed. It can be resolved that it be "left to lie" and the meeting proceeds to the next business.

6.   Closure. This means that the question under discussion should be put to a vote and if carried the debate comes to an end. If it is rejected, the discussion on the matter may continue.

7.   That a matter be referred to a committee. If this motion is carried, then it would be put into the hands of a committee already in existence, or one to be created which may have specialist knowledge to deal with the matter under discussion.

2.   Amendments

An amendment is a variation of a motion. When a speaker proposes an amendment, he can make no further comment on the matter. The amendment must be relevant to the original motion. It must also be positive in nature and similar to the motion. When an amendment is put to the meeting and is accepted by the requisite majority, it is then incorporated into the original motion and it then becomes known as a substantive motion.

The amendments are put in such a way as to give efficacy to the sequence of words in the motion. An example would be that an original motion may state: "that A be appointed to the committee of a club". However, two amendments to this motion are put forward:

1.   that A's period of office will terminate on July 1 of the next calendar year, and

2.   that A be paid £100 expenses per month, while in office.

The method normally used at meetings to deal with such amendments is to put the amendment in such a way as to convey a sense of meaning approximating to the original motion. Therefore, in the example above, the second amendment will be put to the meeting in the first instance and then the first amendment. If both amendments are carried, by way of a vote, they are incorporated into the original motion, which now becomes the substantive motion and reads as follows:

" That A be appointed to a committee of a club. That A will be paid £100 expenses while in office and that A's office will terminate on the next calendar year. This substantive motion is subsequently put to the meeting and voted upon."

If there are two or more amendments relating to the same part of the motion and the meeting carries one of them, the rest, by implication, are rejected. An amendment, which adds further words to a motion, is called an addendum. A rider is a recommendation of some kind after the motion has been carried.

9. Voting

1. Proxies

A proxy is normally appointed where the regulations permit for one member to appoint another to vote on his or her behalf, as provided for by section 136 of the Companies Act 1963.

2. Methods of Voting

There are a number of standard methods of voting, which include the following:
1. Division. This is the method used in the Dáil, where members file into separate lobbies in favour or against a motion.
2. Acclamation. Members are called upon to show their approval by calling out loudly in favour of the motion. This would appear to be the least democratic method of testing the response of a meeting.
3. A show of hands. This is done by the raising of a hand to signify approval or rejection of a motion. If there are objections to what the chairman of a meeting has ascer tained from this type of vote, an objection must be made there and then and a demand for a poll be made.[1]

4. Poll. A poll refers to a method of voting which involves taking a vote at an election, or on a motion. It usually follows a vote on a show of hands. A member may, either in person or by proxy, sign a paper for or against the motion and these votes are counted. The right to demand a poll exists at common law and the only way that this right can be excluded is by the constituted body introducing provisions to do so.[2] If a poll is

---

[1] See *Cornwall v. Woods* (1846) 7 L.T.O.S. 189.
[2] *R. v. Wimbledon Local Board* (1881/1882) 8 Q.B.D. 458.

demanded it should be kept open for a reasonable period to allow all qualified persons entitled to vote.[3]

5. Ballot. A ballot refers to any system of secret voting. A list of candidates' names appear in alphabetical order on the ballot paper and votes are cast in a specified manner whether by single non-transferable vote or by proportional representation.

---

[3] *R. v. St Mary, Lambeth, Rector of* (1838) 8. A.&E. 356.

10. Right to Demand a Poll

There exists at common law a right to demand a poll.[1] This principle was applied in the case of *The Queen v. Wimbledon Local Board*.[2] In this case a meeting of ratepayers was summoned for the purpose of determining whether the provisions of the Public Libraries Act should be adopted in the defendant's district. A chairperson was chosen at the meeting and this was followed by a resolution to adopt the specified Act which was carried on a show of hands. A poll was subsequently demanded, but the chairperson refused to accede to this demand. The defendants declined to put the Act into force. An application for an order of mandamus to compel the defendants to carry out the Act was refused by the court. The court went on to hold that the members had a right, at common law, to demand a poll.

This principle was elaborated on in the case of *Campbell v. Maund*.[3] The court in this case stated that an elector could not be deprived of a right to a demand a poll unless he or she was deprived of such rights by special custom or by the express exclusion of such a right.[4]

Where a body is acting under a statutory duty the power to ask for a poll can only be taken away by the clear words of the statute.[5] When a poll is taken it cancels any vote on a show of hands.[6] The right to demand a poll at a meeting must be made at once as soon as the preliminary show of hands is over. So, in effect, "it is not competent for an elector to lie by and allow all the elections to take place and then demand a poll for some particular township".[7]

The right to demand a poll at a meeting of a company has been given statutory recognition by the Companies Act 1963. Section 137(b) of the Act provides that the right to demand a poll can be made by the following categories of members at a general meeting:

---

[1] *Anthony v. Seger* (1889)1 Hagg. Cons. 9, *per* Lord Stowell.

[2] (1882) 8 Q.B.D. 459.

[3] (1836) 5 A.&E. 865. See judgment of Tindal C.J.

[4] *R. v. How* 33 L.J.M.C. 53.

[5] *Anthony v. Seger*, above, n.1.

[6] *R. v. Vicar of St Asaph* (1883) 52 LJ QB 672 *per* Williams J.

[7] ibid.

(i)   "by not less than five members having the right to vote at the meeting.

(ii)   by a member or members representing not less than one-tenth of the total voting rights of all the members having a right to vote at the meeting.

(iii)   by a member or members holding shares in the company conferring a right to vote at the meeting, being shares on which an aggregate sum has been paid up, equal to not less than one-tenth of the total sum paid up on all shares conferring that right."

Section 137(2) provides: "The instrument appointing a proxy to vote at a meeting of a company shall be deemed also to confer authority to demand or join in demanding a poll..."

11. Majority

There is an established principle at common law that the will of the majority present and voting at a meeting shall prevail on any question.[1]

This principle was applied in the company law case of *Foss v. Harbottle*. Here the directors had been charged with fraudulent and illegal transactions whereby the property of the company had been misapplied and an application by a shareholder was made to the court to appoint a receiver to take over the property of the company. It was held that the courts would not interfere in the internal affairs of a company where the irregularity complained of could be rectified by the company itself.[2] In the circumstances as there was nothing to prevent the company from taking the proceedings if it wished, then the action must fail.

The principle laid down in the case of *Foss v. Harbottle* is to the effect that if there is a wrong done to a company, or if there is an irregularity in its internal management, which can be confirmed by a simple majority of the members, the court will not interfere at the behest of a minority of members. The company itself should take proceedings if the majority of the members decide to do so.[3]

This principle was elaborated on in the case of *MacDoughall v. Gardiner*:

> "if the thing complained of is a thing which in substance the majority of the company are entitled to do, or if something has been done irregularly that the company are entitled to do regularly, or if something has been done illegally which the majority of the company are entitled to do legally, there can be no use in having litigation about it. The ultimate end no doubt is that a meeting has to be called and then ultimately the majority gets its wishes."[4]

---

[1] *Attorney General v. Davy* (1741) 2 A.C.K. 212.

[2] But where the majority propose to gain at the expense of the minority, the courts will interfere to protect the interests of a minority shareholder, see *Meniors v. Hopopers Telegraph Works* (1874) LR 9 Ch. 350.

[3] 1843 - 2 Hake 461.

[4] 1975 1 Ch.D. 13, *per* Mellish L.J.

Four exceptions have been established in regard to the rule of *Foss v. Harbottle*. These give members of a company the right to take proceedings against a company, even though the member is part of a minority of members in the following situations:

1.   The majority cannot commit an act which is illegal or *ultra vires* the powers of the company[5]

2.   Where the company passes a special resolution by means other than the majority as specified.[6]

3.   In the case of an action by a company which interferes with the rights of the share holders.[7]

4.   To prevent a fraud on the minority.

Such a situation was held by the courts to have occurred where the directors of a railway construction company made use of their position to secure for themselves the benefit of a contract for the building of a railway which should have gone to the company. They used their majority voting position to procure the passing of a special resolution to endorse these actions.[8]

There are other examples where a decision by a majority to undertake certain actions have been set aside by the court.

An example of this occurred in *Roper v. Ward*. A social and recreational club owned certain property, which it sold and then proceeded to wind up the club by way of a voluntary liquidation. The management committee decided that non-members would be entitled to a share of the assets of the company when it went into liquidation. The company went into liquidation and the liquidator applied to the court, pursuant to section 280 of the Companies Act 1963 to decide, among other things, if the resolutions passed by the company purporting to give shares in the

---

[5] *Ashbury Railway Carriage and Iron Company Ltd v. Riche* (1875) L.R. 7. H.L. 653.

[6] *Cotter v. National Union of Seamen* [1929] 2 Ch. It was also stated "the position is the same with regard to an extraordinary resolution because both the special and extraordinary resolution require a ³⁄₄ majority and not a simple majority" *per* Romer J.

[7] *Pender v. Lushington* [1877] 6 Ch. 70.

[8] *Cooke v. Deeks* [1916] 1 A.C. 554.

distribution of surplus assets to persons who were not members or associate members were valid and effective. The court decided that the resolution was neither valid nor effective because of a defective notice of the meeting of the company. The members present could not decide that the assets would be distributed otherwise than in accordance with the articles of the company.[9]

It appears that the rule of *Foss v. Horbottle* is not a rigid rule and may be set aside, among other things, where the justice of the case requires it.[10]

An alternative remedy is available to a member of a company where it appears to him that the affairs of a company are being conducted in an oppressive manner. This member may apply for an order to the High Court under section 205(3) of the Companies Act 1963, which provides that: "this subsection may be availed of with a view to bringing to an end the matters complained of, make such order as it thinks fit, whether directing or prohibiting any act or cancelling or varying any transaction or for regulating the conduct of the company's affairs in future, or for the purchase of the shares of any member of the company by other than members of the company or by the company and in the case of a purchase by the company for the reduction accordingly of the company's capital of otherwise."

Section 205 was considered in *Re Westwind Holding Company Ltd.* The company had two members, the petitioner and H, each holding an equal number of shares. H had forged the petitioner's signature in order to execute the sale of the company's property to a company in which he had a substantial interest. N, unknown to the petitioner had lodged the title deeds to more of the company's property, to secure a loan given to another company in which he also had a major interest. To enable him to do this he had to forge the petitioner's signature on the minutes of the director's meetings and on the form lodged when registering the charge pursuant to section 99 of the Companies Act 1963. The court held that the conduct was fraudulent and oppressive and H was ordered to purchase the petitioner's share in the company.[11]

In the case of *Re Williams Group (Tullamore) Ltd.* the board of directors decided that it would be fair to allow preference shareholders to

[9] *Roper V. Ward* [1981] I.L.R.M. 408.

[10] *Moylan v. Irish Whiting Manufacturers Ltd. and others*, unreported, High Court, April 14, 1980.

[11] Unreported, High Court, May 21, 1974.

participate in the accrued profits earned from a particular part of the company's business. To this end, a scheme was devised and passed at a general meeting on May 13, 1985 at which ordinary shareholders were not allowed to attend to allow the distribution of money between all preferential shareholders. A number of ordinary shareholders objected to this matter, they alleged that the action of the preference shareholders was oppressive and had been taken in disregard of their rights. In granting them relief under section 205, Barrington J., referring to *Re Westwind Holdings*, stated: "that an isolated transaction can give rise to relief under Section 205". He continued:

> "It appears to me that the resolutions of the 13.05.1985 were carried out in disregard of the interest of the ordinary shareholders. It appears to me that the implementation of these resolutions is an ongoing matter in the company and justifies the view that the affairs of the company are being conducted in disregard of the interest of the ordinary shareholders. I fully accept that the proposal put forward in the resolution of the 13.05.1985 was put forward in good faith. Nevertheless it appears to me that it is an objective disregard of the interest of the ordinary shareholder and that to persist in implementing it would in the circumstances be oppressive to the ordinary shareholder."[12]

Share Value

O'Hanlon J. approved of the dictum of Oliver L.J. in the case of *Bird Precision Bellows Ltd.*, in the matter of *Clubman Shirts* in reference to section 205(3) of the 1963 Companies Act: "This subsection confers a wide discretion on the court to have regard to all the circumstances of the particular case in assessing at what it considers to be a fair value to be placed on the shares to be acquired."[13]

---

[12] Unreported, High Court, Barrington J., November 8, 1985.
[13] [1983] I.L.R.M. 323.

12. Postponement

The adjournment of a meeting is different from a postponement. A postponement occurs when a meeting is put back before the date fixed for the meeting occurs.

A non-constituted body, having no regulations to the contrary, may adjourn a meeting if it so desires. However, if a postponement is prohibited by the regulations of a constituted body then the meeting may not be validly postponed.

This situation occurred in a case where a general meeting was duly called, but was then postponed to a later date on a date prior to the date for which the meeting was called. A company director due to retire attended with some shareholders that re-elected him as a director. In a court challenge to the decision arrived at, it was held that the resolution reappointing the director was valid as no power was given in the articles to postpone the meeting in question.[1]

---

[1] *Smith v. Paringa Mines* [1906] 2 Ch. 193.

13. Adjournments

An adjournment of a meeting occurs when a meeting is set down for a future date and time. If no date is set down for the adjourned meeting then it is said to be adjourned *sine die*. It would appear that, apart from a limited number of exceptions, the right to adjourn a meeting is a matter to be decided upon by the members of the meeting in attendance.

In a case involving a vestry meeting held to elect church wardens, at which the local vicar presided, the vicar nominated a particular nominee of his choice but, in disagreement with the vicar's choice, the parishioners nominated two other candidates. Prior to the completion of the election of the wardens, the vicar decided to adjourn the meeting despite objection from some members. These members remained on in the hall, after the vicar had left, and elected one of their candidates to be chairperson. The vicar held a subsequent meeting with a group of supporters and proceeded with a poll to elect his nominee.

It was held by the court that the chairperson of a meeting had no inherent right to adjourn the meeting against the wishes of the members. The continuation of the meeting after the departure of the vicar and the subsequent election of the chairperson was held to be valid.[1]

There are, however, certain given situations where a chairperson has an inherent right to adjourn a meeting, *e.g.* to preserve order and to take a vote.

This point was discussed in the case of *R. v. D'Oyly* regarding the right of a rector to adjourn a meeting:

> "Setting aside the inconvenience that might arise if a majority of the parishioners could determine the point of adjournment, we think the person who presides at the meeting is the proper individual to decide this...It is on him that it devolves both to preserve order in the meeting and to regulate the proceedings so as to give all persons entitled to a reasonable opportunity of voting. He is to do acts necessary for these purposes on his own responsibility and subject to being called upon to answer for his

---

[1] *Stoughton v. Reynolds* (1736) 3 Stra 1045 Fort 168.

conduct if he has done anything improperly"[2]

It would appear that apart from the two main exceptions referred to; a chairperson has the general inherent right to adjourn a meeting against the wishes of the members present.

Sometimes the regulations of the body may have provisions permitting the chairperson to adjourn a meeting at his own discretion even if against the wishes of the members present at the meeting.[3]

The regulations may direct that the chairperson must adjourn a meeting when requested by the meeting. In this situation he is left with no option but to adjourn the meeting in question.[4]

It has to be borne in mind that if the chairperson adjourns a meeting, no business shall be dealt with at the adjournment apart from the business being dealt with at the meeting from whence it was adjourned.

---

[2] (1840) 12 A.&E. 139, *per* Lord Denman.

[3] *Salisbury Gold Mining Co. v. Hathorn and ors* [1897] A.C. 268.

[4] Companies Act 1963, s.131(9) which *inter alia*: "gives the company members the right to adjourn the meeting from time to time".

14. Natural Justice and Access to Information

The concept of natural justice is a very important principle in the operation of what are collectively described as fair procedures and can be equated with a duty to act fairly where a person's rights may be affected. The term "natural justice" can be difficult to define precisely.[1]

If a meeting takes on a role of carrying out a judicial or even quasi-judicial function, it must observe certain criteria and it is implicit in that function that it should comply with the rules of fairness and justice. This concept was well elucidated by Barron J. in the following terms:

> "...once a lay tribunal is required to act judicially, the procedures to be adopted by it must be reasonable having regard to this requirement and to the consequences for the person concerned in the event of an adverse decision accordingly, procedures which might afford a sufficient protection to the person in one case, and so be acceptable might not be acceptable in a more serious case..."

In the present case, the principles of natural justice involved relate to the requirement that a person should be made aware of the complaint against him or her and should have an opportunity to prepare and present his or her defence. Matters to be considered are the form in which the complaint should be made; the time to be allowed to the person concerned to prepare a defence; and the nature of the hearing at which that defence may be presented. In addition, depending on the gravity of the matter, the person concerned may be entitled to be represented and may also be entitled to be informed of his or her rights. Clearly, matters of a criminal nature must be treated more seriously than matters of a civil nature but ultimately the criteria must be the consequences for the person concerned of

---

[1] *Calder v. Bull* (1798) 3 U.S. 386 at 399, *per* Iredell J.: "The ideas of natural justice are regulated by no fixed standard, the ablest and porest men having differed on the subject."

an adverse verdict.[2] In *Garvey v. Ireland* O'Higgins C.J stated:

> "The Constitution incorporates into our laws and their adminis-
> tration the requirements of natural justice, and by Article 40, s.3
> there is guaranteed to every citizen whose rights may be
> affected by decisions taken by others the right to fair and just
> procedures. This means that under the constitution powers can
> not be exercised unjustly or unfairly. This applies as well to the
> Government as to any other authority within the state to which
> is given the power to take action which may infringe on the
> rights of others."[3]

In the light of the above statement it would seem quite clearly that administrative bodies dealing with matters which affect a person's rights must
act in a fair and proper manner. This is further underpinned by the
requirements of constitutional justice. The term constitutional justice was
referred to as a concept by Walsh J. in *MacDonald v. Bord na gCon*.[4] In
his judgment he stated that the concept of natural justice could be:

> "...More appropriately termed as Constitutional Justice and must
> be understood to import more than the two well established
> principles that no man shall be a judge in his own cause and *audi
> alteram partem*."

---

[2] *Flannagan v. University College Dublin* [1989] I.R. 724, and see also *Keady v.
Commissioner of an Garda Síochána*, [1990], 2 I.R. 493 at 498, *per* Costello J.: "A distinc-
tion has to be borne in mind between functions and powers of a judicial nature and functions and powers which have to be exercised judicially...the former must be exercised in
Courts of Law, unless they are of a limited character the latter need not...When powers and
functions are impugned because they are of judicial nature and outside the scope of Article
37 it is necessary to consider the legal source of the powers and functions which are being
reviewed, the nature, their object, how they can legally be exercised as well as the consequences which flow from their exercise." Costello J. also commented that the body in question was involved in a decision relating to a disciplinary matter in an important branch of
the public service and the decision was an administrative one based on administrative powers which should be exercised judicially.

[3] [1981] I.R. 76 at 97, and note also the comments made by O'Higgins C.J. in his judge-
ment where he referred to the principles of natural justice as being of two kinds, *nemo iudex
in sua causa* and *audi alteram partem*.

[4] *MacDonald v. Bord Na gCon* [1965] I.R. 217 at 242.

It would appear that the rules of natural justice and constitutional justice require fairness in all proceedings in which a party has a right or interest. The tenets underlying the principles of constitutional and natural justice can be considered under two main headings, namely *audi alteram partem* and *nemo iudex in sua causa*.

1. Audi Alteram Partem [Hear the Other Side]

This effectively means a right to a fair hearing.[5] There is no definitive list of rights that can be implied under the *audi alteram partem* rule. However, we can list a number of important implied rights.

A person is entitled to proper notice of any meeting in which his or her interest may be affected.[6] A similar implied right is the right to meet and to present a case.[7] A former Commissioner of the Garda Síochána was not allowed to answer certain charges levied against him prior to his dismissal by the Government from office. The court held that there was an inherent unfairness of procedure with the processing of his dismissal.

It is an essential principle that fairness of procedure by decision-making bodies should be observed where there is an interference with a person's rights.[8]

Another feature of the *audi alteram partem* rule is the right to legal representation. In the case of *State (Healy) v. Donoghue* it was stated that a person should be afforded an opportunity to be represented by a suitably-qualified person in regard to the matter under discussion.[9]

---

[5] *Calder v. Bull*, above, n.1.

[6] *e.g.* in the case of a prisoner who had been granted several periods of temporary release was refused any further period of release and no reason for the decision was given, see *Sherlock v. Governor of Mountjoy Prison* [1991] I.R. 451. In this case Johnston J. in the High Court directed that the respondent in proceedings by way of judicial review must confront the applicant with the reasons why the temporary release was not renewed and afford to him an opportunity of dealing with the reasons. See also the *State (Gleeson) v. The Minister for Defence* [1976] I.R. 280 and *Young v. The Ladies Imperial Club* [1920] 2 K.B. 523. where it was held that in the cae of a member who was expelled from a club such a member was entitled to notice of the meeting where the matter of her expulsion would be discussed.

[7] In *Re Haughey* [1971] I.R. 217; see also *Garvey v. Ireland*. above n,3.

[8] See *McNellis v. Donegal County Council*, unreported, High Court, December 7, 1978 *per* Darcy J.

[9] [1976] I.R. 325; see also *Re Greyhound Racing Association (No.1)* [1968] 2 All E.R. 545.

2.   *Nemo iudex in sua causa* [no one shall be a judge in their own cause]

It has been stated that: "It is a fundamental rule that it is necessary not alone that justice be done, but that seen to be done".[10]

It is a prerequisite of all proceedings that bias should be excluded by the adjudicating body. A District Court judge disallowed counsel's objection to a Garda reading his evidence from a prepared statement and stated: "The days of the Garda making a slip in the witness box are long gone and if he does make a slip I will recall him." When the garda in the witness box indicated that he was reading from his note book, the respondent advised him not to bother responding to counsel and that counsel was only trying to trip him up.

It was held by Morris J., in granting the relief sought, that the respondent's attitude to the valid objections of counsel was an unwarranted interference with counsel in the performance of his duty; that the suggestion of the respondent that he would recall the garda in the event of his making a slip was improper and unjustified and would cause an impartial observer to recognise that the respondent was prepared to fill in gaps to support the prosecution's case; and that the respondent's actions in calling the garda, whom the prosecution had not called to give evidence when he had already ruled against a dismissal, were an attempt to assist the prosecution by copper-fastening a previous decision.

It was further held that there was a breach of the fundamental rule that not only justice be done but that it should be seen to be done.[11]

It should be noted that it is not necessary to prove that bias actually exists. The important question is whether there are circumstances under which it may well exist. A reasonable apprehension of bias may arise, *e.g.* where a relationship exists between the adjudicating body and a party appearing before it. The effect may be that the person adjudicat-

---

[10] *The State (Hegarty) v. Winters* [1956] I. R. 320 at 336, *per* Maguire C.J.; see also *The People (DPP) v. McGinley*, unreported, Court of Criminal Appeal, November 27, 1989, Hederman J., p.252: "By virtue of the obligation under the Constitution and in order to ensure that justice is done a criminal trial must be held in public and the accused should be present during all of a criminal trial on indictment which includes sentencing. It is not in accordance with law that any part of a criminal trial should be held in a judge's chamber and in the absence of the accused."

[11] *Dineen v. Delap.* 2. [1994] 2 I.R. 228.

ing on the matter could be regarded from a reasonable observation as being both the accuser and arbitrator.[12]

In an English decision bias was held to exist where a social worker involved in adoption proceedings retired with the justices considering the matter. Their verdict was quashed because justice had not been seen to be done.[13]

Another example of where the *nemo iudex* rule was held to have been breached involved the purported removal of a union officer, by vote of the executive of the union, from a meeting of the executive attended by officials having a non-pecuniary interest in establishing the charges against the officer in question. These officials were present at a decisive meeting of the executive at which a decision concerning the officer's position was reached, from which the officer in question was excluded. The decision to dismiss him was held to be void.[14]

If, however, a person attends a meeting which purports to deal with a matter which affects his rights and it appears that the body may be prejudiced or biased, he should object at that particular time. A failure to do so may lead to a conclusion that his right of objection was waived.[15]

Access to Information on Meetings of Public Bodies

Until the enactment of the Freedom of Information Act 1997[16] there was no general right to obtain information regarding meetings of a public body at which decisions were taken except for certain exceptions. An example would be section 3 of the Local Government (Planning and Development) Act 1993 (which amended section 78 of the Local Government (Planning and Development) Act 1963). This provides for the disclosure by way of regulation of the publication by local authorities exercising planning functions, of any proposed development and the provision in this regard of information and documentation to certain speci-

---

12 *O'Reilly v. Cassidy* [1995] 1 I.L.R.M.

13 *Re B. (Adoption by Parents)* [1975] Fam. 129.

14 *National Engineering Union v. McConnell*, Unreported, Supreme Court, December 17, 1982.

15 *Corrigan v. Irish Land Commission* [1977] I.R. 317.

16 The main part of the 1997 Act was brought into effect on the April 21, 1998 and in respect of Health Boards came into effect on October 21, 1998. Section 1(2) states: "that subject to subsection (3) this Act shall come into operation one year after the date of its passing.

fied persons concerning any development that they propose to carry out. There exists at common law a right to inspect certain public documents, *e.g.* the registry of births, marriages and deaths, and wills at probate registries.

The 1997 Act is intended to promote a general right of access for the public to information held by public bodies. This can include meetings and decisions made.[17] There are a number of excluded categories, as well as limitations on access in other areas, from such right to access as set out in Part III of the Act. Examples of these would be meetings of the government; certain matters under deliberation at public bodies; law enforcement and public safety and security; defence and international relations.

A person will normally be required to request in writing to the head of the public body in the first instance to obtain access to information in its possession.

However, it should be borne in mind that certain categories of information are exempt from disclosure.[18]

---

[17] The Freedom of Information Act 1997, Sched. 1 sets out a list of public bodies within the meaning of the Act.

[18] See Part III of the 1997 Act, ss. 19–32, which restrict the information that can be disclosed in regard to public bodies. This can include meetings of the government, certain deliberations of public bodies, functions and negotiations of public bodies. It should also be noted that a person may appeal a refusal to disclose information to the Information Commissioner. It is also provided by s.42 that a person may appeal to the High Court against a decision of a Commissioner.

Part Three: Defamation

15. Defamation

The law of defamation has had a heavy impact on the area of meetings and nowhere is this more reflected than in the ever-increasing number of cases arising from utterances of a defamatory nature made at meetings. Therefore, a thorough knowledge of the law of defamation is essential for those involved in organising meetings.

1.   What is a Defamatory Statement?

There is no precise definition of what constitutes defamation but the following definitions may cast some light on this much litigated area:

> "A defamatory statement is a statement which tends to lower a person in the estimation of right thinking members of society generally or causes him to be shunned or avoided by others, or exposes him to hatred, contempt or ridicule or conveys an imputation on him disparaging of him in his office, profession, trade or business."[1]

Another judicial interpretation of what constitutes a defamatory statement would be: "Whether the statement would lower the Plaintiff in the eyes of the average right-thinking man, if it does so then it is defamatory if untrue."[2]

It is generally accepted that in order that a statement may be considered defamatory, it must lower a person in the estimation of right thinking members of society generally.[3]

This means in the estimation of society generally, and not merely a section of society. But if the words merely bring a person into ridicule in a section of society, which the court does not recognise, then the statement would not be defamatory in this case. An Irish priest instituted pro-

---

[1] *Halsbury's Laws of England* (4th ed.), Vol. 28, para. 10.

[2] *Quigley v. Creation Limited* [1971] I.R. 269.

[3] *ibid.*

ceedings in regard to words, which referred to him as being an informer among a certain criminal class. He argued that among certain classes who were criminal or would sympathise with crime, it exposed him to great odium to be represented as an informer. The court held that the very circumstances which would cause a person to be regarded with disfavour by the criminal classes would raise his character in the eyes of right-thinking people.[4]

2. Causing a Person to be Shunned or Avoided

"To say untruthfully of any woman that she was a victim of rape may well lower her in the eyes of the community by creating an undesirable interest in her and having her exposed to the risk of being shunned or avoided."[5] Or to hinder mankind from associating with him.[6]

3. Ridicule

An article written about the plaintiff, a well-known professional footballer in Dublin, stating that he never used his right foot kicking a ball because he was unable to do so, was held to be defamatory because it exposed him to ridicule.[7]

4. Hatred

In *Parmiter v. Coupland & Another* allegations were made against a mayor of a borough accusing him of partial and corrupt conduct and ignorance of his duties as mayor and Justice of the Peace for the borough.

Baron Parke, in giving a definition of libel in this case, referred to it as being: "A publication without justification or lawful excuse which

---

[4] *Mawe v. Piggott* I.R. 4 C.L. 54 (Com. Pleas) 1869.

[5] *Youssoupoff v. Metro Goldyn Meyer Pictures* (1934) T.L.R. 581.

[6] *Villiers v. Monsley* (1769) 2 Wilson 403.

[7] *Fullam v. Associated Newspapers Limited.* Irish Jurist 1955/1956, Supreme Court.

is calculated to injure the reputation of another by exposing that person to hatred contempt or ridicule."[8]

5.   Libel and Slander

Defamation for historical reasons has been placed in separate categories under the headings of libel and slander. Libel is more permanent in nature and was initially confined to defamatory statements which were in written or printed form.

The definition of libel has now been extended to cover many other forms of media including films, drama, radio, songs, cartoons as well as the reading aloud of a defamatory statement.

Unlike slander, libel is actionable *per se*, without proof of special damage. The following cases will serve to outline the wide-ranging nature of libel.

It is libellous to publish a person's photograph without his permission in such circumstances as to cause injury to his reputation or bring him into ridicule or contempt.[9] The following written statements were all held to be libellous; to write of a plaintiff that he was immoral;[10] to write of a person that he had acted as an informer;[11] to write of a businessman that "he is off";[12] to write a solicitor's letter on behalf of a client which contained defamatory matters not relevant to the occasion was held to be libellous.[13] A report in a newspaper stating, among other things, that the sons of the plaintiffs were vicious and supported by their father's unlawful earnings was held to be libellous.[14]

6.   Libel in Business, Trade, Profession and Office

In order that such statements be actionable they must injure a plaintiff in

---

[8] (1840) M. & W. Report 6.

[9] *Tolley v. Fry & Sons* [1931] A.C. 333.

[10] *Halton v. Jones* [1909] 2 K.B. 444; *Archbishop v. Robeson* 1825 2 Bing 21.

[11] *Wynn v. Quillan* 1899 2 F 322–37 S C.L.R. 234.

[12] *Black v. Holmes* 1 Fox & SM 28 Smith.

[13] *McKeogh v. O'Brien Moran* [1927] Ir. R. 348.

[14] *Kirwan v. Tolley* Cr. & Dix. AB.

his or her business, trade, profession or office. The words must reflect on the personal character or the official, professional or trading reputation of the plaintiff.

In the case of *Le Fanu v. Malcomson* a newspaper article imputed that in some Irish factories cruelty was practised upon some employees. The plaintiffs were the owners of a factory in Ireland. The article was held to be libellous.[15] To write of a tradesman that he used false weights was held to be libellous.[16] A letter written by a Roman Catholic bishop to a priest in his diocese designated the plaintiff, a priest, as a "degraded wretch and should be excommunicated, that he was running all over the country like the spirit of darkness seeking whom he may devour" was held to be libellous.[17]

An allegation against an Irish Taoiseach that he misled the Dáil in a newspaper article was held to be libellous.[18]

There can be no libel of a person's goods unless the imputations reflect on his personal trading characteristics. To write that the books sold by a bookseller were immoral was found to be libellous.[19]

7. Slander

Unlike libel, slander is transitory in nature and is actionable only on proof of special damage. This occurs in the following situations:

1. Slander which imputes unchastity or adultery to any woman or girl. (Defamation Act 1961, section 16.)
2. Slander affecting a person's official professional or business reputation., (Defamation Act 1961, section 19).
3. Slander imputing a criminal offence punishable by death or imprisonment.
4. Slander imputing to a plaintiff a contagious disease.

---

[15] 1848 H.L.C. 637/13 L.T.

[16] *Prior v. Wilson* [1851] 1 C.B. [N.S.] 95.

[17] *Crotty v. McMahon* 1 Jones 465.

[18] *Reynolds v. The Sunday Times*, unreported, 1997.

[19] *Griffith v. Benn* (1911) 27 T.L.R. 346.

8.   Slander which Imputes that a Woman or Girl is Unchaste

The words used by a defendant must be understood to refer to a want of chastity, *e.g.* to say of a woman that she was "of loose character and morals"[20] may well fall within this exception, where the statement is untrue. But if the words were understood to be mere vulgar abuse no action will lie.

9.   Slander Affecting a Person's Official Professional or Business Reputation

The words spoken under this heading must be uttered of the plaintiff in regard to his official, professional or business reputation and not merely in his private capacity.

Office/Occupation

A charge made orally against a church warden that he diverted himself on Sunday when he ought to be in the church implied that he had breached his duty as a Church Warden was held to be actionable.[21]

Profession

Under the heading of slander the allegation must refer to a person in his profession in order to be actionable *per se*. For example, it is slanderous to say of a solicitor that he cheats his clients,[22] or to call a qualified doctor a quack,[23] or to say of a merchant that he cheated in his trade.[24]

[20] *Woolnoth v. Meadows* 1804 5 East 463.
[21] *Moore v. Bloxam* I.R. Term. Rep. 9 F2.
[22] *Jenkins v. Smith* 1621 Cro. Jac. 516.
[23] *Allen v. Eaton* 1630 1 Roll A.B.R.
[24] *Ireland v. Lockwood* 1640 Cro. Carr. 570.

Employment

Oral imputations about the immorality of a civic guard made to his sergeant were held to be actionable *per se*.[25] The words must be spoken of a person in his or her calling.[26]

Trade

To say a person is dishonest is not actionable unless the words are spoken in connection with other slanderous expressions or are connected with some facts or circumstances relating to the exercise by the plaintiff in his or her trade. Allegations against a plaintiff publican that he kept a "hell's gambling den" and sold intoxicating liquor without licence were held to be defamatory.[27]

A person engaged in trade may be defamed if oral allegations are made in regard to the goods, which he or she sells. An example may be where there is an imputation of fraud in the sale of such goods.[28]

The alleged slanderous words must be proven to have been spoken of the plaintiff in his trade. To say of a person "he is dishonest or a rogue" is not actionable *per se* unless the words be spoken in connection with other slanderous expressions or connected with some facts or circumstances relating to the exercise by the plaintiff of his trade.[29]

10. Slander Imputing a Criminal Offence Punishable by Death or Imprisonment

An example of slander under this category could include an oral accusation against a plaintiff of shoplifting.[30] Allegations made by a defendant

---

[25] *Devine v. Keane* 61 I.L.T.R. 118.

[26] *Sayers v. Bachelor* 7 Irish Jurist OS 257.

[27] *Crawford v. Todd* CA N.I. 75 I.L.R.T.

[28] *Foster v. Hood* C.P. VII 92.

[29] *Crawford v Todd*, above, n.27.

[30] *McEntee v. Quinsworth*, unreported, Supreme Court, December 17, 1993.

that the plaintiff was a "pickpocket" were held to be defamatory.[31] It is important to note that, in order for the words to be actionable *per se*, they must impute a crime and not a mere suspicion of one.[32] Imputations such as "you are a swindler or a rogue" are not actionable unless they impute a criminal offence.[33]

11.   Words Imputing Contagious Disease

A spoken statement alleging that a person suffers from a contagious disease is actionable *per se*. An example may be an imputation that a plaintiff suffers from venereal disease.[34]

The disease must be contagious or infectious. The words must refer to the existence of the disease when the words were spoken. False allegations that a person suffers from AIDS or TB could equally be said to come into this category.

In order for the defamatory statement to be actionable it must be an untrue statement.

The defamatory statement must refer to the plaintiff though it does not necessarily follow that the plaintiff should be named specifically.[35]

It is necessary to prove that the defamatory statement refers to the plaintiff in such circumstances to enable those who knew the plaintiff to understand that he was the person meant.

Where the reference is to a limited group the plaintiff may not be able to maintain an action unless he can establish that he was specifically referred to.

An article appeared in an English newspaper that in some Irish Factories cruelties were practised against employees. The plaintiffs were factory workers and were able to prove that they were the parties referred to in the defamatory article.[36]

---

[31] *Henderson v. Boyd* 1857 10 Ir. Jur (NS) 27 EC.

[32] *Frank v. Alsop* 1608 Cro. Jac. 215.

[33] *Black v. Hunt* Q.B.D. XII 24.

[34] *Milner v. Reeves* 1670 1 Roll ABR 43.

[35] *Janson v. Stuart* 178 Ir 748.

[36] *Le Fanu v. Malcolmson*, above, n.15.

Incorporated bodies may sue for defamatory statements made in regard to such bodies.[37]

There can be no defamation of the dead. However, it is a criminal offence to write and publish defamatory words of a deceased person if done with intent to injure and bring contempt on his family and so provoke them to a breach of the peace.[38]

12. Publication of a Defamatory Statement

No action can be maintained in the case of defamation unless there is publication of the statement to a party other than the plaintiff.

If a defamatory letter was sent to a plaintiff's office, there would be publication if the letter was opened and read by a member of the staff even though the letter was sealed.

But if the letter was opened by a servant in breach of his duty there is no publication.[39]

Other examples of publication of a defamatory statement include:

1. Sending an uncovered postcard through the post containing a defamatory statement;[40]
2. Handing a defamatory letter to a clerk to have it typed or copied;[41]
3. Sending a defamatory letter to a plaintiff, which was mistakenly delivered to his brother living at the same address;[42]
4. Reading from a defamatory statement to persons other than the plaintiff constituted a sufficient publication of a libel.[43]

---

[37] *Bognor Regis UDC v. Campaign* [1972] Q.B. 169.

[38] *R v. Ensor* 1873 3 T.L.R. id also *Hilliard v. Penfield Enterprises* [1990] I.R. 138.

[39] *Huth v. Huth* [1915] 3 K.B. 43.

[40] *Sandygrove v. Hole* [1901] 2 Q.B.

[41] *Pullman v. Hill* [1891] 1 Q.B. 524.

[42] *Paul v. Holt* Cs NI 69 I.L.T.R. 157.

[43] *Robinson v. Chambers* [1946] K.B. 82 I.L.T.R.

It was held in *Keogh v. Incorporated Dental Hospital Ireland* that there was no publication where the communication was made by way of private letter to the plaintiff which was opened by the plaintiff's assistant whose practice was to open such letters. Circumstantial evidence was given that the defendant was unaware of this practice.[44]

A verbal accusation of a defamatory nature made by the defendant to the plaintiff on the public street in the presence of on-lookers constituted publication.[45]

Publication of a defamatory statement has been given a statutory format under section 14(2) of the Defamation Act 1961.

13.   Defamatory Statement

"In determining what is a defamatory statement the judge will construe the words in accordance with a fair and natural meaning such as would be given to them by reasonable persons of ordinary intelligence in our own community and that necessarily involves a consideration of the standards of the community and the position of the plaintiff in that community."[46]

Vulgar abuse of itself does not constitute defamation. Words such as "swindler" or "rogue" are not necessarily defamatory.

In deciding what is defamatory what the defendant intended the words to mean is irrelevant. But how the words are actually understood by those to whom they were communicated is what is relevant.[47]

Where a creditor wrote to a debtor on a postcard in the following terms – "if you do not remit by return, the matter will be handed over to our Dublin solicitors" – it was held that the words were incapable of a defamatory meaning.[48]

The onus is on the plaintiff to prove that the words bear the meaning alleged, but where two meanings are possible it would be unreasonable that where there are a number of good interpretations, only

---

[44] [1910] 2 I.R. 166.

[45] *Coleman v. Keane Limited* [1946] Ir. Jur. Rep.

[46] *Quigley v. Creation Limited*, above, n.2.

[47] *Tolley v. Fry & Sons Limited*, above, n.9.

[48] *McCann v. Edinburgh Roperie Sail Cloth Company* (1889) 28 LR Ir 241.

bad ones should be seized upon to give it a defamatory sense.[49]

It is for the judge to determine as a matter of law if the words complained of are capable of bearing a defamatory meaning.[50]

The judge should not withhold a matter from the jury unless he was unsatisfied that it would be wholly unreasonable to attribute a libellous meaning to the words complained of in determining the matter.[51]

14. Defamatory Meaning.

If the judge finds that it is so then he will leave the matter to the jury to decide if the words were in fact understood as being defamatory as published. The court has power and inherent jurisdiction to strike out a case at the preliminary stage where no cause of action was maintained.[52]

15. Innuendo

A publication innocent upon its face may take on a defamatory colouring in the light of extraneous facts when known.[53]

When the defamatory words complained of according to their natural or ordinary meaning convey no meaning, or a meaning which is innocent, the plaintiffs may seek to prove that the statement contains a hidden or secondary meaning, which is of itself defamatory.

> "The question here does not depend on the state of facts known only to a special class in the community, but an inference which could be drawn by the ordinary man and woman from the publication...If it was capable of such a meaning it seems to me that the Judge was bound leave the case to the Jury".[54]

The plaintiff must use evidence to prove that the meaning he ascribes to

---

49 *Nevil v. Fine Art Company* [1895] 2 Q.B. 156.

50 *Capital & Counties Bank v. Henity* (1882) 7 Appeal Cas. 741.

51 *Quigley v. Creation Limited*, above, n.2.

52 *Conlon v. Times Newspapers* [1995] I.L.R.M.; *DK v. AK* [1993] I.L.R.M. 710.

53 *Cassidy v. The Daily Mirror Newspaper* [1929] 2 K.B. 331.

54 *Tolley v. Fry & Sons,* Hailisham V.C., above, n.9.

the innuendo was the meaning in which the words were understood by those to whom they were published. It is not necessary that every person to whom they were published understood them in a defamatory sense. It suffices that some of the addressees understood it in that sense.

For instance, an article which described a married couple as lately having become engaged was found to contain an innuendo that others would have concluded that they were unmarried and cohabiting. The defendant published in a newspaper a photograph of a Mr Corona and a Miss Cassidy together with the words, "Mrs Corrigan whose engagement has just been announced." The plaintiff was known amongst her acquaintances as being the lawful wife of Mr Corrigan, the defendant did not know this.

It was held that the publication was capable of conveying a meaning defamatory of the plaintiff and the jury found that it conveyed to reasonably minded people an aspersion on her moral character.[55]

It is for the court to decide if the words are capable of the meaning alleged in the innuendo. It is for the jury to determine whether the meaning was properly attached to them.[56]

Defences to an Action for Defamation

Justification

It is clear that the truth of a libel supports a complete answer to civil proceedings. The defence of justification is based on the grounds that the words are true in substance and in fact.

To sustain the defence of justification the defendant has to prove, not only that the facts are truly stated, but also that any comments upon them are correct.[57] So, from a practical point of view, if a defendant alleges that a plaintiff was convicted of a crime, he must prove that this is so.

If a person repeats a rumour, he cannot say it is true by proving the truth of the rumour. A charge of general bad conduct cannot be justi-

---

[55] *Cassidy v. The Daily Mirror Newspaper*, above, n.53.

[56] *Australia Newspaper Company v. Bennett* [1894] A.C. 284.

[57] *Sutherland v. Stopes* [1925] A.C. 47.

fied by proof of a single act or instance.[58]

Under such a plea of justification a defendant must prove the truth of all the material statements in the defamation not merely the facts, but also the comments on the facts.

Under such a plea, it is not necessary to prove the truth of every word of the libel, if a defendant succeeds in proving that "the main charge or gist of the libel is true". He need not justify statements or comments which do not add to the sting of the charge.

A statement that the plaintiff had been convicted of travelling in a train without a ticket and was fined £1.00 with three weeks' imprisonment on default of payment, was held to be justified by proof that he had been fined £1.00 for that offence with a fortnight imprisonment in default of payment.[59]

The plea of justification has been given a statutory format in section 2 of the Defamation Act 1961:

"In an action for libel or slander in respect of words containing two or more distinct charges against the plaintiff, a defence of justification shall not fail by reason only that the truth of every charge is not proved if the words not proved to be true do not materially injure the plaintiff's reputation, having regard to the truth of the remaining charges."

There is a danger in relying on a defence of justification as a failure to prove the truth of either facts or comments may aggravate the damages being awarded.

Fair Comment

The defence of fair comment applies to comments made on matters of public interest where public persons are involved. The comments do not necessarily have to be true, but the facts on which the comments rest must be truly stated and such facts must exist at the time of publication. The facts must not be contrived or fabricated.

The comments must not be an imputation of corrupt or dishonourable motives, unless such imputation is warranted by the facts truly

---

[58] *Wakely v. Cook* Exch. Vol. 2, 511; see also *O'Brien v. Bryant* 1846 MW. & W. 168.
[59] *Alexander v. NE Ry Co.* 1865 6 B.&S. 34.

stated or referred to and the inference is one which a fair-minded man may reasonably draw and thereby representing the honest opinion of the writer.

It was held to be actionable to suggest, however honestly made, that the editor of a religious magazine, in advocating a scheme for missions to the heathens, was in reality an impostor inspired by pecuniary motives. The court found that this went beyond an ordinary criticism of the plaintiff as the author of his book.[60]

Malice will defeat a defence based on fair comment so that comments on the facts must be fairly and honestly made and if not so, malice may be inferred from the comment.[61]

17.   Statement of Fact

The question that must be asked is whether the allegation is a comment or a statement of fact.

If a defendant alleges gross behaviour against a public figure, but does not state what this behaviour is, that is a statement of fact. This could occur in an allegation made by the plaintiff that the defendant conspired against him.[62] If the writer gives an honest expression of his real opinion and the facts are truly stated, the comment will not necessarily be unfair if the views of the critic were exaggerated, incorrect, or prejudiced. But criticism cannot be used as a cloak for mere invective.[63]

Private character or conduct of such persons who hold public office or take part in public office may be subject to fair comment if the activity referred to in the comment relates to the performance of duties or fitness to hold office.

But the private lives of public persons, with which the public has no concern, is not within the domain of fair comment.[64]

In regard to fair comment the judge will decide if the matter is of public interest. The jury will decide if the words complained of are allegations of fact or an expression of opinion and if the expression of

---

[60] *Campbell v. Spottiswoode* (1863) B&S 769.

[61] *Sutherland v. Stopes,* above, n.57.

[62] *London Artists v. Littler* [1969] 2 Q.B. 375.

[63] *McQuire v. Western Morning News* [1902] 2 K.B. 109.

[64] *Gray v. S.P.C.A.* 1890 17 R. 1185 & 27 I.R. 906 Ct. of Sessions.

opinion is fair comment or not.[65]

The proof required in the defence of fair comment is that a matter is of public interest. If the statement contains facts, the facts must be proven to be true. It is necessary to prove also that there is no misstatement of the material facts upon which the comment was based. The defendant must also prove that the comment is warranted in the sense that a fair-minded person bona fide held the opinion expressed on them.

18. Public Meetings

In order that a report of a public meeting be privileged, the report must be fair and accurate.[66]

19. Absolute Privilege

Absolute privilege affords a complete defence to an action for defamation. The privilege attaches to utterances and reports of the proceedings of the Dáil and Seanad and proceedings of a judicial or quasi-judicial body.

The privilege also attaches to communication made between certain officers of state and the relationship of solicitor and client.

20. Dáil and Seanad

All utterances in the Dáil or Seanad and official reports or publications from these bodies are absolutely privileged.[67] It is debatable whether a statement made by a person going to or coming from the Dáil would be privileged.

The privilege also attaches to Dáil committees and all statements

---

[65] *Sutherland v. Stopes*, above, n.57.
[66] *Daly v. Cork Herald* 31 I.L.T. 165 and 4 I.L.T.R. 35.
[67] See Art. 15.12 and Art. 15.13 of the Constitution of 1937.

made before these bodies and all documentary records of such proceedings.[68]

21.   Judicial Proceedings

Absolute privilege will apply to statements made during the course of judicial proceedings and official reports of such proceedings. This privilege attaches to statements made by judges, lawyers, witnesses and parties involved in the proceedings and all official reports of the proceedings of such bodies.[69]

Comments which are irrelevant made in the course of judicial proceedings by witnesses are also privileged. It is safe to assume that absolute privilege attaches to utterances of a defamatory nature made in the course of an enquiry of a judicial nature.[70]

Newspaper and broadcast reports of court proceedings have statutory protection pursuant to section 18 of the Defamation Act 1961:

> " A fair and accurate report published in any newspaper, or broadcast by means of wireless telegraphy as part of any programme or service provided by means of a broadcasting station within the State or Northern Ireland, of proceedings publicly heard before any court established by law and exercising judicial authority within the State or in Northern Ireland, shall, if published contemporaneously with such proceedings, be privileged."

The word "absolute" is not used in this section but it appears to be accepted in principle.

The privilege will not extend to a report on any document not opened to the court in the course of judicial proceedings.[71]

A person's dress or demeanour is not part of judicial proceedings and will not attract the privilege.

Section 18 of the Defamation Act 1961 provides that a report of

---

[68] Committee of the House of the Oireachtas (Privileges and Procedure) Act 1976, s.2.

[69] *Mcauley v. Wyse Power* [1943] 77 I.L.T.R.

[70] *O'Connor v. Waldron* 1935 A.C. 76 at 81.

[71] *Stringer v. Irish Times Limited* [1995] 2 I.R. 159.

judicial proceedings must be made contemporaneously with the proceedings "that is as near the time of proceedings as reasonably possible taking into account the opportunity for preparing the reports and of going to press or making a broadcast".

In order that a report may be privileged, it must be fair and accurate.

A newspaper report stated that a Police Constable Lee had accepted a bribe, describing him as Detective Lee; two other officers of the same name were in the police force. It was held that the privilege did not apply to the report.[72]

A slight inaccuracy in the report of judicial proceedings will not necessarily defeat the privilege, provided the report was transcribed without notice of the error or negligence or malice.[73]

The publication must be accurate and without inference of comment.[74]

Privilege will not attach to statements made subsequent to judicial proceedings in a court of law.

22. Qualified Privilege

In regard to the law of meetings, qualified privilege may apply in a situation where directors in a company or a management body may be obliged to discuss a fellow director or worker and in so doing may make a defamatory statement about such a person. In that situation the privilege may attach to the statement made. In order that the privilege may be availed of, there must exist in the person making it a legal or social interest to convey the statement and the person to whom it was communicated has a reciprocating duty or interest to receive it.

In order that a statement shall be privileged, there must be a mutuality of interest in the making and receiving of it.[75] It is not required that both parties have a duty or that both parties have an interest, as one party may have an interest and the other party may have a duty, *e.g.* in a situation where a servant is being employed.

[72] *Newstead v. London Express Newspapers Limited* [1940] 1 K.B. 377.

[73] *Annally v. Trade Auxilarry Company* Ed. XXIV/29 C.A. XXIV.

[74] *McNally v. Oldham* [1863] Q.B. I.C.C.R. 298.

[75] *Redmond v. Kelly* Ex 28 I.L.T. 555.

23.   Duty

An example of duty was found to exist where a plaintiff made oral allegations to police officers regarding the plaintiff concerning a matter under investigation in which the defendant had an interest. It was held that the words were spoken on a privileged occasion.[76]

Where a letter of complaint was sent to the Incorporated Law Society, in which it was alleged that the plaintiff had accepted a retainer from the defendant in an action then pending and afterwards took the opposite side in the same case, it was held to be privileged and that apart from a social duty the defendant had sufficient interest in the matter under complaint.[77]

The defendant in exercising his duty must keep it within its proper bounds as any excess on his part will be frowned upon by the courts.

In *Sevenoaks v. Latimer* a postmaster, in the course of enquiries which he had been instructed to make by the post office in regard to the misappropriation of a postal order, made a statement to another party at a premises where the plaintiff had subsequently been employed of his belief that the plaintiff had been guilty of the crime under investigation. It was held by the court that the statement was not made on a privileged occasion. It was no part of the defendant's duty to make such a statement and the third party had no interest in the matter complained of.[78]

24.   Interest

Certain statements may be privileged if made in the protection of an interest. This matter was considered in the case of *Pyke v. Hibernian Bank*. A cheque was drawn by a customer in favour of a third party. The customer's account had sufficient funds to meet the cheque. Upon presentation of the cheque by the payee, it was returned by the bank endorsed with the words "refer to drawers and present again". It was held that the communication was made in the bona fide exercise of an interest which exist-

---

[76] *McFadden v. Lynch* (1883)17 I.R.L.T. 93.

[77] *Kirkwood Hackett v. Tierney* [1952] I.R. 185, 88 I.L.T.R.

[78] K.B. Div 54 I.L.T.R.

ed in the defendant and in the party receiving the communications. It was also held that the occasion was privileged.[79]

In protecting an interest the defendant should refrain from using excessive methods in dealing with the matter—pursuing and confronting a suspected shoplifter on the street with an accusation of having committed a theft.

In a case where words were spoken for the purpose of recovering articles believed to be stolen or of obtaining payment for them which was not actuated by a desire to cause the arrest and prosecution of a suspected criminal, the claim of privilege was disallowed.[80]

Qualified privilege is a limited defence and may be defeated by proving the existence of malice.

25. Malice

The existence of malice will undermine a defence of qualified privilege. Malice means using a privileged occasion for some ulterior motive other than a sense of duty.[81] Carelessness will not constitute malice if the defendant honestly believed the truth of the statement though having no reasonable grounds for such belief.[82]

Malice may be gleaned from an assessment of the general behaviour of the defendant, *e.g.* a statement against a plaintiff in a state of anger; being reckless or careless as to the truth of the statement; ill-will, spite or threats against the plaintiff or comments that are irrelevant to the duty or interest at issue.

26. Undue Publication

Malice may also be gleaned from undue publication which means publishing a statement to a party with no interest in the matter, calling into an office a third party to hear a defamatory statement in which he has no interest; or raising a voice so loudly that persons with no interest in the

---

[79] [1950] I.R. 195.

[80] *Coleman v. Keane*, above, n.45.

[81] *Hooper v. Truscott* 1836 3 Bing N.C.

[82] *Browne v. Hawkes* [1891] 2 Q.B. 722.

matter can hear what is being said. These acts may constitute malice, as may accusing a customer of shoplifting, in a public street.[83]

Malice will also be established if a defamatory statement is made at a shareholders' meeting by a defendant to which he has invited members of the public and the press.[84]

If the press was present as of custom at a meeting at which the defendant made his defamatory remark, malice will not be inferred.[85]

Malice will not be inferred from the fact that a defamatory but privileged statement was accidentally overheard or if the privileged statement was dictated to a typist in the reasonable and ordinary course of business.

Certain newspaper reports are privileged as set out in section 24 of the Defamation Act 1961, which states:

> "(1)   Subject to the provisions of this section, the publication in a newspaper or the broadcasting by means of wireless telegraphy as part of any programme or service provided by means of a broadcasting station within the State or in Northern Ireland of any such report or other matter as is mentioned in the Second Schedule to this Act shall be privileged unless the publication or broadcasting is proved to be made with malice.

> (2)   In an action for libel in respect of the publication or broadcasting of any such report or matter as is mentioned in Part II of the Second Schedule to this Act the provisions of this section shall not be a defence if it is proved that the defendant has been requested by the plaintiff to publish in the newspaper in which the original publication was made or to broadcast from the broadcasting station from which the original broadcast was made, whichever is the case, a reasonable statement by way of explanation or contradiction and had refused or neglected to do so, or had done in a

---

[83] *Coleman v. Keane*, above, n.45.

[84] *Parsons v. Surgey* 1864 4 F.&F. 247.

[85] *Pittard v. Oliver* [1891] 1 Q.B. 474.

manner not adequate or not reasonable having regard to all the circumstances.[86]

(3)   Nothing in this section shall be construed as protecting the publication or broadcasting of any matter the publication or broadcasting of which is prohibited by law, or of any matter which is not of public concern and the publication or broadcasting of which is not for the public benefit.

(4)   Nothing in this section shall be construed as limiting or abridging any privilege subsisting (otherwise than by virtue of section 4 of the Law of Libel Amendment Act, 1888) immediately before the commencement of this Act."

27.   Offer of Amends

Section 21 of the Defamation Act 1961 recognises the concept of an offer of amends:

"If a defendant has published words which he alleges to be defamatory of another person he may claim that the words were published innocently regarding another person. If the offer is accepted by the aggrieved party and is duly performed, no proceedings for libel or slander shall be taken or continued by that party against a person making the offer in respect of publication in question (but without prejudice to any cause of action against any other person jointly responsible for the publi cation).

An offer of amends shall be understood to mean (individual or joint) publication of a suitable correction of words complained of and sufficient apology to the party aggrieved in respect of these words."

---

[86] *Nevin v. Roddy and Carty* [1935] Ir. R. 397.

28.   Consent

Where a plaintiff gives consent to the publishing of an alleged defamatory statement, this constitutes a good defence to any action instituted by the plaintiff against the defendant. Such a consent may be contained in a contract entered into by a plaintiff subsequent to the publishing of the statement.

Consent may be also deduced from a given situation outside the area of contract on the basis of *volenti non fit injuria*. An example of this would be to invite the defendant to repeat the statement in front of others.[87]

Where an investigation committee relied on the defence of consent by a plaintiff to the publication of a statement of complaint and details of the investigation, it has been held that the committee had to prove that it supplied the plaintiff with a copy of its rules prior to the investigation.[88]

Malice will defeat a defence based on consent. Malice may be implied if a statement was published from a wrong motive which amounted to malice. An example of malice was found to exist where an investigation committee acted outside its jurisdiction in carrying out the investigation, failed to provide the plaintiffs with reasonable notice of the complaint to be answered or provided an opportunity to be heard. It was held to have failed to comply with the rules of natural justice.[89]

Malice may be implied if a statement was given an unnecessary wide publication, e.g. publishing a statement to persons with no interest in the matter.

29.   Apology

An apology is not a defence to an action for defamation, but it is admissible in evidence in mitigation of damages in an action for defamation.[90]

---

[87] *Chapman v. Ellesmere* [1932] 2 K.B. 431.

[88] *Reilly v. Gill & ors* 85 I.L.T.R. 165.

[89] *Green v. Blake & ors* [1948] I.R. 242.

[90] Defamation Act 1961, s.17.

30. Defamation Act 1961

Second Schedule

Statements Having Qualified Privilege

Part 1
Statements Privileged without Explanation or Contradiction

1. A fair and accurate report of any proceedings in public of a house of any legislature (including subordinate or federal legislatures) of any foreign sovereign State or any body which is part of such legislature or any body duly appointed by or under the legislature or executive of such State to hold a public inquiry on a matter of public importance.

2. A fair and accurate report of any proceedings in public of an international organisation of which the State or Government is a member or of any international conference to which the Government sends a representative.

3. A fair and accurate report of any proceedings in public of the International Court of Justice and any other judicial or arbitral tribunal deciding matters in dispute between States.

4. A fair and accurate report of any proceedings before a Court (including a courtmartial) exercising jurisdiction under the law of any legislature (including subordinate or federal legislatures) of any foreign sovereign State.

5. A fair and accurate copy or extract from any register kept in pursuance of any law which is open to inspection by the public or of any other document which is required by law to be open to inspection by the public.

6. Any notice or advertisement published by or on the authority of any court in the State or in Northern Ireland or any Judge or officer of such a court.

Part II

Statements privileged subject to Explanation or Contradiction

1.   A fair and accurate report of the findings or decision of any of the following associations, whether formed in the State or Northern Ireland or of any committee or governing body thereof, that is to say: -

   (a)   an association for the purpose of promoting or encouraging the exercise of or interest in any art, science, religion or learning and empowered by its constitution to exercise control over or adjudicate upon matters of interest or concern to the association or the actions or conduct of any person subject to such control or adjudication;

   (b)   an association for the purpose of promoting or safeguarding the interests of any trade, business, industry or profession or of the persons carrying on or engaged in any trade, business, industry or profession and empowered by its constitution to exercise control over or adjudicate upon matters connected with the trade, business, industry or profession or the actions or the conduct of those persons;

   (c)   an association for the purpose of promoting or safeguarding the interests of any game, sport or pastime, to the playing or exercise of which members of the public are invited or admitted, and empowered by its constitution to exercise control over or adjudicate upon persons connected with or taking part in the game, sport or pastime;
   being a finding or decision relating to a person who is a member of or is subject by virtue or any contract to the control of the association.

2.   A fair and accurate report of the proceedings at any public meeting held in the State or Northern Ireland, being a meeting

bona fide and lawfully held for a lawful purpose and for the furtherance of discussion of any matter of public concern whether the admission to the meeting is general or restricted.

3.   A fair and accurate report of the proceedings at any meeting or sitting of -

    (a)   any local authority, or committee of a local authority or local authorities, and any corresponding authority, or committee thereof, in Northern Ireland;

    (b)   any Judge or Justice acting otherwise than as a court exercising judicial authority and any corresponding person so acting in Northern Ireland;

    (c)   any commission, tribunal, committee or person appointed, whether in the State or Northern Ireland, for the purposes of any inquiry under statutory authority;

    (d)   any person appointed by a local authority to hold a local inquiry in pursuance of an Act of the Oireachtas and any person appointed by a corresponding authority in Northern Ireland to hold a local inquiry in pursuance of statutory authority;

    (e)   any other tribunal, board, committee or body constituted by or under, and exercising functions under statutory authority, whether in the State or Northern Ireland;

Not being a meeting or sitting admission to which is not allowed to representatives of the press and other members of the public.

4.   A fair and accurate report of the proceedings at a general meeting, whether in the State or Northern Ireland, of any company or association constituted, registered or certified by or under statutory authority or incorporated by charter, not being, in the case of a company in the State, a private company within the meaning of the Companies Act, 1908 to 1959, or, in the case

of a company in Northern Ireland, a private company for the time being in force therein.

5.   A copy or fair and accurate report or the summary of any notice or other matter issued for the information of the public by or on behalf of any Government department, local authority or the Commissioner of the Garda Síochána or by or on behalf of a corresponding department authority or officer in Northern Ireland.

Part Four: Local Authorities and Meetings

16. Local Authorities and Meetings

In the Republic of Ireland there are a number of types of local authority body. These include county councils, county boroughs, borough councils, town commissioners and urban district councils. Many of the statutory provisions relating to meetings and procedures of local authorities may be amended and/or substantially repealed by the Minister for the Environment, by way of regulation, under section 30 of the Local Government Act 1994. This section in the 1994 Act has not yet been brought into force by the Minister.

1.   County Councils

County councils were established under the Local Government (Ireland) Act 1898.[1] Every county council shall hold an annual meeting in every year in which a quinquennial (five-year term) election to a county council is held.[2] The annual meeting should be held at noon on the fourteenth day after the day of the election, and in every other year the annual meeting of the council will be held 14 days either before or after the anniversary of the first annual meeting, as the council appoints.[3]

---

[1] Section 1 of the 1898 Act states: "A Council shall be established in every administrative County and be entrusted with the management of the administrative and financial business of that county and shall consist of a chairman and Councillors". See also the Local Government (Reorganisation) Act 1985 which created three new electoral counties: Fingal, Belgard (South County Dublin), Dun Laoghaire-Rathdown.

[2] See Local Elections Act 1966, s.1(1) which states *inter alia* that: "An election of members of every local authority shall be held in the year 1967 and quinquenially thereafter." However, note that ss. 30 (1), (2) and (3) of Part V of the Local Government Act 1994 (which has not yet been substantially brought into effect) provides that the Minister for the Environment may make provisions in relation to meetings and procedures of local authorities.

[3] The original provisions for the dates of annual and quarterly meetings, contained in s.8(1) of the 1927 Act, were not repealed and were carried over by the 1966 Act for the period of 1966. See also S.I. No. 128 of 1965 which states: "an annual meeting in any election year shall be held 14 days after polling day and in a year other than election year, the annual meeting shall be held either before or after the anniversary of the first annual meeting as the Council appoints".

Whenever an annual or quarterly meeting of a county council is, for any reason, not held on the day appointed, the clerk or secretary must summon a meeting for a day and time that appears convenient for the purpose of this meeting. This shall be deemed to be an annual meeting.[4] The county councils are obliged to hold four quarterly meetings in the year between the annual meeting and June 1, as they decide or as prescribed in their standing orders.[5] The chairperson may at any time call a meeting of the council. If the chairperson refuses to call a meeting after a requisition for that purpose, signed by at least five members of the council and presented to him or her, any five members of the council may themselves call such a meeting.

If the chairperson, without making a refusal, does not call a meeting within seven days of this being presented, then any five members of the council may, after the expiration of the seven days, call a meeting. This provision allows essential business to be discussed by the council.[6]

The County Management Act 1940 provides that estimate meetings must be held by the county council annually. This is another meeting which is obligatory in accordance with statute law and ensures that the issue of funding for the following financial year is addressed. The preparation of estimates may be carried out by the manager or by the estimates committee established under section 7 of the City and County Management (Amendment) Act 1955.

If no committee has been appointed or if such committee fails to prepare the accounts, then the manager must do so. When they are prepared, a copy must be sent to each member of the local authority and must also be made available to members of the public for inspection. The estimate of expenses must be adopted by a resolution of the local authority.

The members of the local authority may amend the estimates at the estimates meeting, or any adjournment of the meeting within the following 20 days. The period for the preparation and holding of the estimates meeting must occur between October 1 and December 21 in every year.[7] The meetings and procedures regarding estimates are similar for all local authority bodies.

---

[4] See S.I. No. 128 of 1965, art. 82.

[5] Schedule to the Application of Enactment Order 1898, art. 10, s.4.

[6] Schedule to the Application of Enactment Order 1898, art. 10, s.4.

[7] Public Bodies (Amendment) Order 1992, S.I. No. 327. These provisions are applicable to all local authority bodies.

2.   Notice of Meetings

Three clear days of notice must be given for any meeting of the council, which is called by the chairperson, specifying the time and place of the intended meeting, and must be signed by the chairperson. But if the meeting is one called by the members of the council on requisition by the members, it must be signed by those members and a notice to this effect should be fixed at the place where the council normally meets.[8]

In every other instance, three clear days of notice of any meeting of the council must be given and should state the business to be dealt with and be signed by the secretary. This notice shall be sent to the address of every member of the council.[9] The validity of a meeting shall not be affected by a failure to serve such notice.[10]

No business shall be transacted at a meeting other than that specified in the summons, except in the case of an annual meeting involving the election of a chairperson.[11]

3.   Election of Chairperson

The first business to be transacted at an annual meeting of a county council shall be the election of the chairperson and vice-chairperson.[12] There is a special procedure for the election of a chairperson specified by section 43(1) of the Local Government Act 1941:

"(a)   the proceedings shall begin by a member or members being proposed and seconded and no person who is not then proposed and seconded shall be a candidate;

(b)   where there is only one candidate, such candidate shall be elected;

---

[8] Schedule to the Application of the Enactment Order 1898, art. 10(3)(v): "where the meeting is called by the members of the Council, it shall state the business to be dealt with".

[9] *ibid.,* art. 10(3)(vi).

[10] *ibid.,* art. 10(3)(vii).

[11] See the Local Elections Act 1966. The election of a county pensions officer without notice was held to be void: *R (Fitzgerald) v. McDonald* [1913] 2 I.R. 55.

[12] Local Elections Regulations, S.I. No. 128 of 1965, reg. 83.

(c)   where there are more than two candidates, a poll shall be taken;
(d)   if at such poll a majority of the members present vote for any particular candidate, such candidate shall be elected;
(e)   if at such poll no candidate receives the votes of a majority of the members present, the candidate receiving the least number of votes shall be eliminated and, subject to the provisions of paragraph (g) of this sub-section, one or more further polls, according as may be necessary, shall be taken;
(f)   paragraph (d) and (e) of this sub-section shall apply in relation to such further poll or polls;
(g)   where there are only two candidates or where, as a result of one or more polls taken under this sub-section, all the candidates except two have been eliminated, the question as to which of such candidates shall be elected shall be put to the members present and whichever candidate of such receives the greater number of votes on such question shall be elected;
(h)   if from an equality of votes given to two or more candidates any question arises under this sub-section as to which of such candidates is to be eliminated or as to which of such candidates is to be elected, such question shall be decided by lot."

The next business of an annual meeting shall be the appointment or nomination of the members of joint committees or joint boards.[13]

4.   Role of the Chairperson[14]

At every meeting of the council, the chairperson, if present, shall chair the meeting. In the absence of the chairperson, the vice-chairperson assumes this role. If the chairperson dies, then the vice-chairperson is also entitled to sit as chairperson (but without a casting vote).[15] If a chairperson commits an illegal act, the members may elect another chairperson in his or her place without breaking the continuity of the meeting.

---

[13] S.I. No. 128 of 1965, art. 84(1).

[14] The Local Government Act 1994, s.25(1) states that there shall be a Cathaoirleach and Leas-Cathaoirleach for each county Council which shall replace the title and style of Chairman. There are other provisions in ss. 25 – 29 governing this office; however, these sections have not been brought into force to date.

[15] *R (Curran) v. Brennan* [1916] 50 I.L.T.R. 68.

Every county council chairperson is entitled to request and be afforded all such information as may be in the possession of the county manager, under section 27 the County Management Act 1940.[16]

If the chairperson is a not a member of the council, he or she shall not be entitled to vote in the first instance or have a casting vote.[17] However, there is another occasion when a chairperson may not exercise a casting vote. This could also occur on the election of a chairperson.[18]

All acts of the council, and all questions coming before the council, may be done and decided by the majority of such members of the council as are present and vote at a meeting. The enactments affected are those which require the assent of the majority present, not those which require the presence of a certain proportion of members.[19] The names of the members present, as well as those voting on each question, must be recorded to show whether each vote given was for or against the question.[20]

5.   Minutes

Minutes of the proceedings should be drawn up and entered in a book kept for that purpose and signed.[21] Minutes of the proceedings at any meeting of the council or committee, which are signed at that meeting or the subsequent meeting by the chairperson (or a member of the council or committee who was chairperson at that particular time), shall be received

---

[16] *Cullen v. Wicklow County Manager* [1996] 3 I.R. 474, [1997] 1 I.L.R.M. 41, *per* McCracken J.

[17] Local Government Act 1946, s.6. This section may create difficulty because a chairperson may not be re-elected and still be a member of the council according to Article 83 of S.I. No. 128 of 1965. This specifies that a chairperson elected at an annual meeting subject to the exceptions contained in these regulations remains in office until his successor is elected.

[18] See the Local Government Act 1941, s.43.

[19] *e.g.* the so-called section 4 resolution pursuant to the City and County Management (Amendment) Act 1955, which requires such a resolution to be passed by one third of the membership. See also sections 12 and 14 of the Local Government (Ireland) Act 1902 regarding a resolution to the Minister for Local Government to alter the day of a meeting or section 6(2) of the County Management Act 1940 regarding the suspension or removal of the county manager.

[20] Application of Enactments Order 1898, art. 10.

[21] *ibid.*, art. 13.

in evidence without further proof.[22] Accurate minutes of the proceedings of a council meeting should be kept. The minute book will constitute evidence of what actually took place at the meeting.[23]

6. Quorum

The quorum required for meetings of a county council is ordinarily one quarter of the whole number of the council.[24]

A meeting may be abandoned due to lack of quorum. If a meeting of a county council is abandoned because of a failure to obtain a quorum, the names of the members attending at that time and place shall be recorded and they shall be deemed to have attended the meeting. This is effectively a record of attendance should the question of disqualification arise, for example, for non-attendance.[25]

7. Place of Meeting

Meetings can be held in the county or outside it, wherever the council directs. However, a meeting shall not be held in a licensed premises except where no other suitable room is available either free of charge or at a reasonable cost.[26]

8. County Managers and Meetings

A county manager has a right to attend meetings of the county council and to take part in discussions at meetings but will not be entitled to vote. The county manager may give advice to any council body or committee. A county manager must attend a meeting of the council when he or she is requested to do so and this provision relates also to other committees and meetings of elective bodies of which he or she is manager. The county

---

[22] Application of Enactments Order 1898, art. 8.

[23] *ibid.*, art. 23.

[24] Schedule to the Application of Enactments Order 1898.

[25] Local Government Act 1925, s.64.

[26] Local Government (Ireland) Act 1898, s.77; Application of Enactments Order 1898, arts. 35, 36; see also County Management Act 1955, s.100.

manager deals only with executive matters; reserved matters are within the domain of the council. He or she also has a function in the preparation of estimates following an estimates meeting.[27] In certain local authority areas the county manager acts in dual capacity as both city and county manager.

9.   Standing Orders

Standing orders are the rules and procedures which may be drawn up by a county council to facilitate the smooth running of its meetings. Article XIV of the Schedule to the Application of Enactments Order 1898 provides that the council may from time to time make standing orders for the regulation of its proceedings and business and vary or revoke them.[28] Standing orders must not be *ultra vires* the powers of the authority in question.[29]

10.   Admission of the Press to County Council Meetings

Section 15 of the Local Government (Ireland) Act 1902 states that:

> "No resolution of any council, board or commissioners to exclude from its meetings representatives of the press shall be valid unless sanctioned by the minister for local government in pursuance of by-laws, which the Minister for Local Government is empowered to frame regulating the admission of the press to such meetings.[30]

---

[27] County Management Act 1940, s.30(1), (2).

[28] Local Government Act 1955, s.62(1) states that a local authority may make standing orders for the regulation of their proceedings outside those which are governed by statutes. However, it should be noted that this provision would appear to have not been implemented to date. For further discussion see *McNelis v. Donegal County Council*, unreported, High Court, Darcy J., December 7, 1978.

[29] *R v. Downing* 1886 16 L.R. Ir. 501.

[30] See H.A. Street on Local Government (Stationery Office on behalf of the Incorporated Council of Law Reporting), p.76.

Members of the public have no general right to attend county council meetings.[31] However, in practice members of the public often attend these meetings, subject to the right of council members to exclude them at any time by going into committees or otherwise.

11. Committees

A county council may delegate matters to committees which are concerned with the exercise or performance of any of their powers, duties or functions. The committees can be general, dealing with a range of matters relating to the whole of the county, or local, dealing only with part of the county. The procedures and functions of committees and joint committees are now covered by Part VI of the Local Government Act 1991, sections 36–40.[32]

All committees must have at least three members who may include members of the council or non-members (with particular expertise, for example). These committees are subject to the jurisdiction of the council.

The council may make regulations for the conduct and procedure of committee meetings. A council may not delegate powers to a committee where this is prohibited by law or statute, or where the functions are of an executive nature which fall within the ambit of the county manager.[33]

Where there is an equal division of votes on any matter at a meeting of a committee, the chairperson shall have a second or casting vote. The election of a chairperson in the case of equality of votes is determined by lots.[34]

The process for voting and other matters in relation to council committees is similar to that pertaining to the council body as a whole. There are provisions which provide that committees may, in some cir-

---

[31] *Tenby Corporation v. Mason* [1908] 1 Ch. 457.

[32] This part of the Act is concerned with the appointment of committees of local authorities. These include committees of a general nature, joint committees and the membership and qualifications of the members appointed.

[33] Local Government Act 1925, s.58 and County Management Act 1940, s.18(2).

[34] Local Government Act 1946, s.63(1), (2).

cumstances, be designated as local authorities.[35] The provisions regarding the retirement of members of a joint committee or council are dealt with by the Local Election (Amendment) Regulations of 1974,[36] regulation 2 of which provides that retirement (subject to certain exceptions specified) shall occur the day after the annual meeting or quarterly meeting of such local authority after election.

12. Retirement

The ordinary day of retirement for members of a local authority is seven days after polling day or, in the case of a situation occurring where an election is countermanded, interrupted, or adjourned, after the day on which the poll is complete.[37]

13. Disqualification[38]

Persons can be disqualified from becoming members of a county council or remaining in such capacity on a number of specified grounds. These include:

1. being under 18 years of age;

2. having being convicted, before or since election, of a crime and sentenced to imprisonment with hard labour, without the option of a fine, or to any greater punishment and not having received a free pardon;[39]

---

[35] Local Government Act 1941, s.2(2)(6).

[36] S.I. No. 117 of 1974.

[37] Local Election Regulations 1965, reg.85, S.I. No. 128 of 1965.

[38] Local Government Act 1994, s.6(1) extends the categories of public office holders who are precluded from local authority membership and also certain other categories of persons. However, these provisions were due to come into force at the local elections for 1999. See also section 6(4) of the 1994 Act.

[39] Application of Enactments Order 1898, art. 12.

3. conviction for having knowingly acted as a member when disqualified;[40]

4. being absent from meetings for a disqualifying period, unless the absence is due to illness or for reasons approved by the council. The period averred to is 12 months in the case of a county council;[41]

5. being members of the defence forces on the active list;[42]

6. failing to pay rates before the end of the financial year for which they are due;[43]

7. failing to pay local government auditor charges;[44]

8. making false claims for expenses.[45]

It should be noted that the provisions regarding disqualification of members apply to all local authorities and their respective committees.

14. Disclosure of Interests

There are statutory safeguards against possible conflicts of interest for members of local authorities. These include having a pecuniary or beneficial interest in matters pertaining to planning decisions.[46] Council members are obliged to disclose any interest they have in lands within the council's planning area and also any business dealing in or developing lands with which they are engaged or employed. There is a similar statutory provision regarding persons voting as members of a housing author-

---

[40] Local Government Act 1925, s.60.
[41] Application of Enactments Order 1898, art. 12.
[42] Defence Act 1954, s.104.
[43] Local Government Act 1941, s.57.
[44] Local Government Act 1925, s.62.
[45] Application of Enactments Order 1898, and the Local Elections (Petitions and Disqualifications) Act 1974, s.24.
[46] Local Government (Planning and Development) Act 1976, ss.32, 33.

ity or on certain committees in relation to any house or land in which they have an interest.[47]

15. Boroughs

Before dealing with meetings and procedures of such bodies it is instructive to describe their origins. Prior to the passing of the Municipal Corporations (Ireland) Act 1840 there were four boroughs in existence, namely Dublin, Cork, Limerick and Waterford. These were created by royal charter and were given a specific title under section 12 of the 1840 Act.

There were a number of other boroughs whose bodies were given statutory recognition pursuant to section 12 of the 1840 Act and which were listed in the Schedule. It was further provided that after the first election of a councillor in any borough named in Schedule A such a person would be described as "the Mayor, Aldermen, and Burgesses of such borough except the Corporation of Dublin which shall bear the name of the Right Honourable the Lord Mayor, Aldermen, and Burgesses of Dublin".[48]

Section 14 of the 1840 Act created a procedure permitting the inhabitants of those towns listed in Schedule B, and any other town whose population exceeded 3,000, to apply by way of petition to the Minister for Local Government for a charter of incorporation as a borough.[49]

When the Local Government (Ireland) Act 1898 was enacted there were six boroughs. Section 21 of the 1898 Act provided that each of the boroughs referred to in the Schedule of the 1898 Act – namely Dublin, Cork, Limerick and Waterford – became an administrative county and be titled a county borough".

Section 21(2) of the 1898 Act provided that the mayor, aldermen and burgesses of each county borough acting by the council would have all the powers and duties of a county council. It also provided that other

---

[47] Housing Act 1966, s.115.

[48] See s.25 of the Local Government Act 1994, which makes provisions for the altering of these styles and titles which await being brought into force by the Minister for the Environment.

[49] *e.g.* the Borough of Wexford. However, note that s.14 of the Municipal Corporation Act 1840 will be repealed when the Local Government Act 1994 is fully implemented.

boroughs which existed prior to 1898 and whose corporations had been given statutory recognition were permitted to acquire the status of a county borough. If these boroughs did not become county boroughs, they became part of the administrative county to which they were attached.[50]

16. Meetings of Borough Councils and County Boroughs

Every year a county borough should hold four quarterly meetings and an estimate meeting. There is no statutory provision for the holding of annual meetings. It is provided by regulation 81(1) of the Local Election Regulations 1965[50a] that in every year in which an election is held, a quarterly meeting of a county borough or borough corporation shall be "held on the 10th day after the polling day or where the poll is for any reason countermanded, interrupted or adjourned, the day after the poll is completed or the fresh poll is held".

In non-election years the borough is obliged to hold a quarterly meeting, not less than 14 days either before or after the anniversary of the first quarterly meeting, as those bodies by resolution decide.[51] Once the chairperson is elected, joint committees are appointed by the council.

Whenever a quarterly meeting is, for any reason, not held on the day appointed, the clerk or secretary, as the case may be, must summon a meeting of that body at a convenient time and day. This meeting would be deemed the appropriate quarterly meeting.[52] The mayor or lord mayor has the power to call a meeting of the council as often as he or she thinks proper. If the mayor refuses to call a meeting which was requisitioned by five members of the council and which was presented to him or her, the five members may call a meeting of the council. An estimate meeting should be held every year. The provisions for such meetings are similar to those of the county councils.

---

[50] *e.g.* the Borough of Drogheda did not become a county borough and so it became part of the administrative region of County Louth.

[50a] S.I. No. 128 of 1965.

[51] These provisions may be amended by the Minister for the Environment by way of regulation pursuant to section 30 of the Local Government Act 1994, whenever the same is brought into force.

[52] s.82.

17.   Notice

Notice of the time and place of a meeting shall be given at least three clear days before the meeting by fixing the notice on or near the door of the town hall of the borough and notice shall be signed by the mayor.

In the case of a meeting called by the members, three clear days of notice in writing must be given of such meeting and signed by the five members in question, stating the business to be transacted at the meeting. The meeting must be confined to that business.

In every case, a summons to attend a council meeting should specify the business proposed to be transacted and be signed by the town clerk. This should be left at the usual place of abode of every member of the council or at the premises in respect of which he or she is enrolled as a burgess or is qualified to vote.[53] The only business transacted at the meeting is to be that which is stated in the notice.[54]

All decisions may be taken at a duly constituted meeting by a majority of the members present who vote on any matter.[55] However, some meetings require a proportion of members to be present and this could arise in the case of a borough council making by-laws.[56]

18.   The Election of Mayor

The first business at a quarterly meeting, after deciding which members shall be aldermen, will be the election of the lord mayor or mayor, as the case may be.

The mayor shall come into office when he or she has made the appropriate declaration accepting office and shall remain in office until a

---

[53] Municipal Corporation (Ireland) Act 1840, s.92.

[54] See above, n.11, for similar provisions that apply to county councils.

[55] See Local Government Act 1941, s.41(a), (b).

[56] s.125 of the Municipal Corporations (Ireland) Act 1840 clearly stated that no by-laws could be made unless two thirds of the council were present at the meeting where this was being done. However, s.125 of the 1840 Act appears to have been repealed by the Local Government Act 1994 and, while this has been replaced by provisions regarding the enactment of by-laws in Pt. VII of the 1994 Act, it now appears that at a meeting for the making of by-laws the matter may be decided by the votes of a majority of members present.

successor has been elected.[57] There is a special procedure for the election of mayor.[58]

19. Presiding at a Meeting

All acts authorised or required under the Municipal Corporations (Ireland) Act 1840 and all adjournments may be decided by the majority of the members present.[59] However, some questions require a specific proportion of members to be present.[60] At all meetings the mayor, if present shall preside. In the absence of the mayor the members present shall select a chairperson from the aldermen or councillors present (in that order). In all cases of equality of votes the chairperson shall have a casting vote.[61]

20. Minutes of Borough Councils

Minutes of all meetings are obliged to be drawn up and entered into a book retained for that purpose and signed by the person presiding at that meeting.

The minutes should be kept open for inspection to any burgess or voter who is entitled to copies for a specified fee.[62]

---

[57] Local Election Regulations 1965, reg.83.

[58] The procedure for the election of a mayor is similar to that adopted for the election of the chairperson of a county council. See s.43 of the Local Government Act 1941, which provides for the election of a mayor by way of lot; however, pursuant to s.25(3) of the Local Government Act 1994 the mayor in future will bear the title Cathaoirleach, though retaining the title and style of mayor or lord mayor as the case may be.

[59] Municipal Corporations (Ireland) Act 1840, s.92, which must be read in conjunction with s.41 of the Local Government Act 1941.

[60] See s.125 of the 1840 Act, above, n.56, which requires two thirds of the members to be present to vote on the making of by-laws.

[61] However, a chairperson may have a second or casting vote as specified in s.92 of the 1840 Act, except where he is not a member of the council as stated in s.62 of the Local Government Act 1946 or where the question of the election of the chairperson arises as set out in s.43 of the Local Government Act 1941.

[62] It is to be noted that new provisions governing this matter remain to be introduced by the Minister for the Environment pursuant to s.30 of the Local Government Act 1994.

21. Quorums

In the case of borough councils (other than Dún Laoghaire) the quorum was stated to be one quarter of the total number of members of the council. This provision was contained in section 23(2) of the Local Government (Ireland) Act 1898, now repealed by the Local Government Act 1994. However, new provisions in this regard have not been introduced under section 30(f) of the 1994 Act. It would appear that currently the only rules concerning quorums are contained in the standing orders of the various borough councils.

The quorum for Dún Laoghaire borough council is five.[63] The quorum for the county borough of Galway is four.[64] In the case of Cork the quorum was ten, pursuant to the Cork City Management Act 1929 which was repealed by the Local Government Act 1994; there have been no new provisions introduced. The quorum for Waterford county borough was seven, but the Waterford City Management Act has been repealed by the Local Government Act 1994. In the case of Limerick county borough the quorum was seven pursuant to the Limerick City Management Act 1934, similarly repealed by the 1994 Act. As in the case of Cork there appears to be no specific statutory quorum pending implementation of specific regulations by the Minister for the Environment under section 30 of the 1994 Act. Therefore, as in the case of most borough councils, county boroughs are currently guided by their standing orders in relation to quorums.

22. The Right to Appoint Committees

The various boroughs have the right to appoint joint committees and joint boards. This would be in cases when such action is considered necessary. However, such bodies shall not be delegated executive functions which are within the ambit of the county or city manager, as the case may be.[65]

---

63 Dublin Electoral Centres Order, S.I. No. 133 of 1985.

64 Local Government (Reorganisation) Act 1985.

65 Local Election Regulations, s.84(1), S.I. No. 128 of 1965, and s.102 of the Municipal Corporations (Ireland) Act 1840.

23. Attendance of Manager at Meetings

A manager has the right to attend meetings of a local authority and to take part in discussions as though he or she were a member, but without the right to vote. A manager of a borough council or county borough is obliged to attend any meetings of the council or committee of the council whenever requested to do so by that body. The manager must, when attending such a meeting, give advice and assistance. If necessary he or she may have to arrange for the attendance of other officials of the local authority to assist and advise the members.[66] The office of a city manager may be held by the county manager as there is provision for one person to hold both offices.

24. Place of Meetings

The provisions here are similar to those applicable to county councils in relation to holding meetings on licensed premises. But, unlike county councils, borough councils hold their meetings outside the county as the provisions contained in article 36 of the Schedule to the Enactments Order 1898 do not appear to apply to borough councils.

25. The Right of the Public to Attend Meetings

The right of the public to attend meetings of borough councils, contained in rule 31 of the Procedure of Council Order 1899 and section 167 of the Grand Jury Act 1836, is now defunct.[67]

---

[66] County Management Act 1940, s.31.

[67] H.A. Street, *The Law Relating to Local Government* (1955), p.52.

26. The Right of the Press to Attend Meetings of a Borough Council

The press has no absolute right to attend meetings of a borough council,[68] but this may be facilitated by the standing orders of the relevant body. However, any difficulties regarding the rights of the press to attend meetings of borough councils may be remedied when the provisions of the Local Government Act 1994 are fully implemented.

27. Disqualifications

There are provisions governing disqualification from membership of borough councils which are of a similar nature to those applicable to county councils.[69]

28. Urban District Councils

Urban district councils derive their origin from bodies known as urban sanitary authorities, which are defined by section 4 of the Public Health Act 1878 as being of six types:

1. Boroughs inclusive of county boroughs which became urban sanitary districts pursuant to section 4 of the Public Health Act 1878.
2. Towns with a population of 6,000 or more.
3. Towns having commissioners under local Acts.
4. Towns which petitioned under section 7 of the Public Health Act 1878 and were constituted urban districts by a provisional order confirmed by Parliament.
5. Towns which petitioned under section 7 of the Public Health Act 1878 and which by virtue of the Act were confirmed as urban

---

[68] The Local Government Act 1902 (which has now been repealed by the Local Government Act 1994), which provided for the right of the press to attend meetings of certain local authorities, had no application in regard to borough councils. Provisions in this regard remain to be introduced pursuant to s.30 of the Local Government Act 1994.

[69] See disqualification from membership of county councils discussed above at p.100.

districts without confirmation by an order of Parliament.

6.   New boroughs which had the powers of an urban district by statute.[70]

Section 22 of the Local Government (Ireland) Act 1878 provided that all urban sanitary authorities were called urban district councils and their districts were called urban districts. But this section did not interfere with the style or the title of the corporation or council of a borough.

The first meetings of an urban district council are obliged to be held on the tenth day after the day on which polling occurs or if the poll is for any reason countermanded, interrupted, or adjourned, after the day on which the poll is completed or a fresh poll is held.[71] Whenever an annual meeting of the council is for any reason not held on the day appointed under these regulations, the clerk or secretary must summon a meeting of the council at a reasonable time on the earliest convenient date and this meeting will be regarded as an annual meeting.

In every other quinquennial[72] year the council is obliged to hold an annual meeting on such a day being not less than 14 days before or after the anniversary of its first annual meeting.[73] A monthly meeting must be held on the first Monday at 12 noon at an appointed venue.[74] The council may also hold special meetings and any five or more of the members may requisition such a special meeting to be held, but this kind of meeting requires not less than two clear days of notice.[75]

---

[70] *e.g.* Dún Laoghaire.

[71] Local Election Regulations 1965, S.I. No. 1281 of 1965, art. 81(1) which provides: that where The Town Improvement Act has been adopted in whole or part by a town and elections held in pursuance of section 21 of that Act, the Commissioners returned at such election shall on the first Monday after such election hold their first meeting in the town.

[72] s.20(1)(a) of the Local Government Act 1994; see the Local Government Act 1994 (Commencement) No. (2) Order 1995.

[73] Local Election Regulations 1965, Reg. 81 (2).

[74] s.27 of the Towns Improvement Act 1854, this section has been repealed by virtue of the Local Government Act 1994; however, the implementing provisions have not been brought into effect at time of writing. The current practice of holding a monthly meeting reflects the repealed statutory provisions in this area.

[75] s.45 of the Commissioner Clauses Act 1847.

29.   Notice

In the case of an ordinary monthly meeting no notice is required.[76] Where
any business other than ordinary business is to be transacted at a monthly meeting, the clerk shall give notice of this and no such extraordinary
business nor any rules or regulations shall be adopted at a monthly meeting unless notice has been given at the previous meeting and sent to each
member in the manner set down.[77]

No resolution at any meeting of the urban district council shall
be revoked or altered at any meeting unless notice is given by the clerk to
each member at least seven days before the holding of the meeting and
any alteration should be determined by a majority consisting of two thirds
of the members present at such meeting.[78]

Notice shall be in writing or print, or both. The clerk shall serve
notice by delivering it by post or otherwise to the usual place of abode or
place of business of each member. The notice should state the time and
place of the meeting and, in the case of a special meeting, the object of
the business. No business shall be transacted at any special meeting
except as stated in the notice.[79]

30.   Chairperson

The first business at the annual meeting is the election of a chairperson
and vice-chairperson. A chairperson shall continue in office, unless he or
she is disqualified, dies, resigns or is removed from office, or until a successor has been elected.[80] The rules for election of a chairperson are prescribed by the Local Government Act 1941. The method used is by way
of lot (a type of lottery) in the case of equality of votes for the candidates.
The chairperson, who is a member of the council, has a casting vote in

---

[76] *ibid.*, s.40.
[77] *ibid.*, s.43.[78] *ibid.*, s.44.
[79] *ibid.*, s.47.
[80] Local Election Regulations 1965, art.82.

addition to his or her own vote. Matters shall be decided by the votes of the majority of the members present and voting.[81]

Meetings shall be presided over by the chairperson of the council; if he or she is absent, then the vice-chairperson presides. If he or she ceases to be a member, the members may elect one of their number to be chairperson.[82]

The members of the council must make a record of all proceedings, which is kept by the clerk under the superintendence of the members and signed by the chairperson of the meeting at which the proceedings took place. This signed entry will be received in evidence in all courts. No further proof of the meeting having being duly convened or held or that persons attending were members or that the signature is the chairperson's is required; all of these shall be presumed until the contrary is proven. The records must be available for inspection to all members.

The Public Bodies Act 1946 provides that accurate minutes are to be kept of the proceedings of every local authority.

31. Quorum

The quorum of an urban district council is one quarter of the total membership of such council.[83]

32. Place of Meeting

Urban district councillors shall hold their first general meeting in the town hall, or other convenient place in the town, as they nominate, with a power to adjourn to any place they think fit.[84]

Meetings of town commissioners and urban district councillors, which have adopted the provisions of the Towns Improvement (Ireland) Act 1854, will hold their first meeting in any convenient place in the

---

[81] Local Government Act 1941, s.41. There are meetings which require a certain proportion of members to be in attendance. An example of this would arise in the case of revoking a resolution of the council, which requires a majority of two thirds of the members present at the meeting. See section 44 of the Commissioners Clauses Act 1847.

[82] Commissioners Clauses Act 1847, s.37.

[83] Local Government (Ireland) Act 1898, s.23(2).

[84] Towns Improvement (Ireland) Act 1854, s.27.

town. However, they may not hold their meetings on a licensed premises or club which sells alcohol unless there are no other suitable rooms available either free of charge or at a reasonable cost.[85]

33. Admission of the Press to District Council Meetings

The provisions governing the right of the press and members of the public are similar to those which govern meetings of county councils as are applicable. This includes the holding of an estimate meeting.

34. Commissioners

Meetings of town commissioners are similar to those of urban district councils. The statutory provisions that govern meetings of town commissioners are to be found substantially in the Commissioners Clauses Act 1847.

The quorum for a meeting of the commissioners of a town which is not an urban district is three.[86] Meetings of town commissioners may be held on licensed premises if necessary.

At all meetings of the commissioners questions shall be decided by the votes of the majority of the members present and if there is an equal division of votes on any question, the chairperson or commissioner acting as chairperson shall, in addition to his or her own vote, have a second or casting vote, except in the election of a chairperson.[87]

34. Section 4 Resolutions

Section 29 of the Local Government Act 1940 gives certain powers of control to elected members over the manager in discharge of his or her function. The City and County Management (Amendment) Act 1955 enables a manager to perform a function *intra vires* his or her powers.

---

[85] Local Government (Ireland) Act 1898, s.77.

[86] Local Government Act 1946, s.66.

[87] Commissioners Clauses Act 1847, s.38; see also s.43 of the Local Government Act 1941.

This type of a resolution is called a section 4 resolution.

Section 4(1) of the City and County Management (Amendment) Act 1955 provides that a local authority may, by resolution, require performance of any particular act or thing specifically mentioned in the resolution which the local authority or the manager can lawfully do.

Notice of the intention to propose such resolution must be given in writing to the manager and be signed by three members of the council. The notice must specify a day not less than seven days after the receipt of the notice by the manager for the holding of the meeting at which the resolution is to be considered. It must be passed at least by one third of the total number of members.[88]

---

[88] City and County Management (Amendment) Act 1955, s.4(6).

17. Local Authority Committees

There exist at present a number of local authority committees which are constituted by statute. The two main areas in which such committees exist are in the fields of education and agriculture. The procedures for meetings of these bodies are invariably regulated by the various statutes and standing orders.

1.   Vocational Education Committees

This type of committee was established by the Vocational Education Act 1930 in every local authority area. The title and style of these committees varies somewhat in the different local authority areas but their function and procedures are generally of a similar nature.[1]

The vocational education committee for a borough vocational educational area shall comprise 14 members elected by the council of the county borough, of whom no fewer than five and no more than eight shall be members of such a council.[2]

It is further provided that where such a vocational area contains more than one urban district which are not scheduled urban districts, and the membership of each urban district does not exceed four, then two of the members selected by the council may, at their discretion, be non-members of the council appointing that committee.

If the membership of such urban districts exceeds four, then one of those members appointed may be a non-member of the council.[3]

The rules governing appointments of non-local authority members to the Vocational Education Committees are governed by rules set out in Schedule 5, Part 2 of the Local Government (Reorganisation) Act 1985.

---

[1] s.6(1) of the Vocational Educational Act 1930 provides that "every borough shall be a borough vocational committee". s.6(2) states that every scheduled urban district shall be an urban district vocational education area, and s.3 provides that every county (apart from those included in the scheduled urban district) shall be a county vocational area.

[2] Vocational Education Act 1930, s.8(3)(a).

[3] *ibid.*, s.8(3)(b)(i), (ii).

Rule 4 states that where only one person is to be appointed, he or she shall be appointed by a majority of the votes of the members of the local authority present at the meeting of the authority when such appointments are being made. Rule 5 states that in the case of two or more persons failing to be appointed to such committee they shall be appointed under the following provisions:

1. Rule 5 (a) states that any group of members may nominate a person to be a member of that committee and the person nominated shall be then appointed without the necessity of a vote.

2. Rule 5 (b) provides that the remaining members of the committee shall be elected by majority vote of the members of the relevant local authority.[4]

There are provisions in the Act for the inclusion on such committees of members who have been recommended by the various employer/employee associations involved in manufacturing or trade within the committee area and also persons with interest and experience in education.[5]

2. Appointment to Committees

In every year the council of a county or urban district which is not a borough council shall elect members to the Vocational Education Committee at its annual meeting and, in the case of a borough council, these appointments shall be made at the quarterly meeting.[6]

A member of a committee shall remain in office (unless he or she dies, resigns or becomes disqualified to be a member of such committee) until the next meeting at which the local authority is required to elect a new committee.[7]

---

[4] Local Government (Reorganisation) Act 1985, Sched. 5, Pt II, clauses 4-6.

[5] Vocational Education Act 1930, s.8(4).

[6] *ibid.*, s.9(2)(a), (b).

[7] *ibid.*, s.10(2), (3).

3.   Meetings

It is provided in the Act that the committee shall hold one meeting in each month, except in July, August and September. They must also hold at least one meeting between July 1 and September 30 in each year and they may hold such other meetings at such times and places as they require. Every Vocational Education Committee must also, in each financial year and before December 1 of that year, hold an annual meeting.[8]

Every Vocational Education Committee shall on or before May 31 in every election year appoint a day for a meeting, not being earlier and not later than 10 days after completion of such election.[9] Where no day has been appointed for the holding of such a quinquennial[10] meeting, then it shall be the seventh day after completion of the election in that particular year.[11]

If a quinquennial meeting of a Vocational Education Committee is not held for any reason (including a quorum not being present) on the day appointed, the chief executive officer of such a committee shall summon a meeting of the committee at what appears to him or her to be the earliest convenient date.[12]

4.   Chairperson

It is provided by the Act that every Vocational Education Committee shall, at its first meeting and every quinquennial meeting, elect one of its members to be chairperson.[13]

If there is an election for chairperson consisting of two or more candidates, the chairperson will be elected by lot.[14] When the chairperson is present at a meeting, he or she shall be the chairperson. If the chairperson is absent, then the vice-chairperson shall take his or her place; and if

---

[8] Vocational Education Act 1930, s.13(3).
[9] *ibid.*, s.14.
[10] Every five years.
[11] Vocational Education Act 1930, s.13(3).
[12] *ibid.*, s.14(4).
[13] *ibid.*, s.15(1).
[14] Local Government Act 1946, s.63(1).

neither the chairperson nor the vice-chairperson is present, then the members of the committee may choose one of their own number to be chairperson.[15] The quorum for such committee shall be one quarter of the total membership of such committee.[16]

Every question shall be decided by the majority of members present and voting[17] and in the case of equality of votes the chairperson shall have a second or casting vote,[18] except on the election of a chairperson.[19]

A Vocational Education Committee may act despite the fact that there exists at the time one or more vacancies in its membership.[20]

An inspector shall have the right to attend meetings of the committee and take part in any discussion, but he or she may not vote on any matter.[21]

5. Minutes

Every Vocational Education Committee shall keep a minute book of all proceedings occurring at a meeting and the minutes must be signed at the meeting to which they relate or at the next meeting. When they are signed, the minutes are admitted as evidence of that meeting so held.[22]

6. Sub Committees

The Vocational Education Committee and the Minister shall have the right to appoint sub committees which consist of members who are not members of the committee. Such committees shall consist of no more than 12 members.[23]

---

[15] Vocational Education Act 1930, s.18(2).

[16] *ibid.*, s.18(1).

[17] *ibid.*, s.18(3).

[18] *ibid.*

[19] Local Government Act 1946, s.14.

[20] Vocational Education Act 1930, s.18(4).

[21] *ibid.*, s.18(5).

[22] *ibid.*, s.20.

[23] *ibid.*, s.21.

7.   Casual Vacancies

Whenever a casual vacancy occurs the committee must as conveniently as possible elect a person to fill the vacancy. In regard to casual vacancies in the County of Dublin or the Dun Laoghaire Vocational Education Committees, the following statutory provisions are applicable:

Regulation 3

> "If a casual vacancy occurs before the election of Councils of Counties next after the commencement of the regulations, the Vocational Education Committee concerned, following consultations with the Minister for Education, has the power to select a person to fill the vacancy and upon selection, that person shall become and be a member of the Vocational Education Committee.

Regulation 4

> "Having regard to the provisions relating to the composition of such committees set in selecting a member to fill a casual vacancy a Vocational Education Committee shall set out in Section 8 (3) of the 1930 Act and shall ensure that as far as practicable the person selected has an interest and experience in education similar to the member he or she is replacing and if the member whose death, resignation or disqualification, caused the vacancy was originally recommended under Section 8(4) of that Act by any particular body, that body shall recommend someone to fill the vacancy."[24]

8.   Lack of Quorum

Whenever a meeting of the committee is abandoned owing to a failure to obtain a quorum, the names of the members attending at the time are recorded for the purpose of the Act relating to disqualification arising

---

[24] Vocational Education Committees (Filling of Casual Vacancies) Regulations 1996, S.I. No. 205 of 1996.

from a failure to attend meetings and in regard to expenses paid to committee members. A meeting of such a committee shall be deemed to have been held at that time and place and the members whose names are recorded shall be deemed to have attended such meeting.[25]

It is provided by the Act that a committee can make standing orders to regulate its proceedings but these are subject to any statutory regulations which prevail at the time.[26]

9. Committees of Agriculture

The Committees of Agriculture are regulated by the Agriculture Act 1931, as amended by the Agriculture (An Comhairle Oiliúna Talmhaíochta) Act 1979, the Local Government (Reorganisation) Act 1985 and various statutory instruments.

The Committees of Agriculture were established by the 1931 Act which provided that such a committee shall be appointed by a council of a county.[27]

The numbers constituting such committees shall be not less than three times nor more than four times the number of county electoral areas in the county at the time of the annual meeting.[28]

Where the number of committee members is divisible by five, three-fifths of the committee shall be chosen by the council.[29]

Every member of such committee other than those members chosen by the council shall be appointed on the nomination of such voluntary rural organisations which are active in the county as the Minister

---

[25] The 1930 Act, s.19.

[26] *ibid.*, s.18(7).

[27] Agriculture Act 1931, s.15.

[28] s.3 of the 1931 Act, but see Sched. 2, clause 26 of the Agriculture Act 1979 which provides that the members of the committee shall be four times the number of county electoral areas at the time of the meeting. See also s.26 of the Local Government (Reorganisation) Act 1985, which specified that these provisions were to apply to·designated counties. Such counties are listed in the Local Government (Reorganisation) Act 1985 (Committees of Agriculture) Order 1985, S.I. No. 131 of 1985 - Dublin, Clare, Cork, Kerry, Kildare, Kilkenny, Laoighis, Louth, Roscommon, Sligo, Westmeath, Wicklow.

[29] Agriculture Act 1931, as amended by Agriculture Act 1979, s.26(1).

stipulates as having such a right of appointment.[30]

Every person appointed to be a member of a Committee of Agriculture shall be chosen or nominated by reason of his or her attainment in farming, or the development of agriculture or the promotion of agricultural or rural home advice or education or by reason of a practical commercial or technical knowledge of agriculture or a special local knowledge of agricultural matters.[31]

A committee shall not be deemed to be invalidly constituted because of a failure of the rural organisation as designated or the council to elect the specified numbers.[32]

10.　Procedures Governing the Appointment of Committees[33]

Among the first item of business to be dealt with at an annual meeting held in an election year shall be the appointing of members to a Committee.[34]

1.　The persons to whose appointment the Second Schedule, rule 2(2) of the 1931 Act applies, namely members nominated by voluntary rural organisations, shall be the first to be appointed.

2.　The next members appointed are those specified in section 4 of the 1931 Act, namely residents from the relevant county, by majority vote.

3.　The remaining members shall be appointed pursuant to the rules of Part II, Schedule 5 of the Local Government (Reorganisation) Act 1985.

4.　Where one person remains to be appointed, he or she shall be appointed by a majority vote.

5.　If two or more remain to be appointed, then the following provisions apply: any group of members may nominate a person

---

[30] Schedule 2, which relates to the appointment and membership of committees of agriculture pursuant to the Agriculture Act 1931, was amended by s.26 of the Agriculture (An Comhairle Oiliúna Talmhaíochta) Act 1979.

[31] Agriculture Act 1931, Sched. 2, r. 5, as substituted by s.26(1)(c) of the 1979 Act.

[32] *ibid.*, r. 6(2), as substituted by s.26(1)(d) of the 1979 Act.

[33] These procedures are governed by Parts 1 and 2 of Schedule 5 of the Local Government (Reorganisation) Act 1985.

[34] Agriculture Act 1931, Sched. 2, r. 6, as substituted by s.26(1)(d) of the 1979 Act.

to be a member of a committee and he or she shall be elected without voting.[35] The last group to be appointed are those members of the council who do not belong to a group; these are appointed successively by majority votes.[36]

11.   Chairperson

The committee shall elect a chairperson who, in the event of an equality of votes occurring on any matter, shall have a second or casting vote, except on the election of a chairperson.[37]

The chairperson in any election contest where there are two or more candidates who receive equal number of votes shall be elected by lot.[38]

12.   Presiding at a Meeting

At any meeting of a Committee of Agriculture the Chairperson, if present, shall be chairperson. If the chairperson of such committee is not present or if that office is vacant, then the vice-chairperson, if present, shall be chairperson. If neither the chairperson nor vice-chairperson is present, the members can select one of their members to be chairperson.[39]

13.   Quorum

The quorum of a Committee of Agriculture shall be four members.[40]

---

[35] Local Government (Reorganisation) Act 1985, Sched. 5, Pt II, cl.5(a).
[36] *ibid.*, cl.5(b) for groups.
[37] The 1931 Act, s.16(3) and Local Government Act 1946, s.64.
[38] Local Government Act 1946, s.63(1).
[39] The 1931 Act, s.16(3).
[40] *ibid.*, s.16(1).

14. Abandonment for Want of Quorum

Whenever a meeting of a Committee of Agriculture is abandoned owing to a failure to obtain a quorum, the names of the members attending at the time and place of the meeting shall be recorded, for the sake of concerns relating to disqualification due to absence from meetings and in regard to travelling expenses and the meeting shall be deemed to have been held at that time and place. The members whose names have been recorded shall be deemed to have attended that meeting.[41]

15. Period of Membership

A member of the committee shall remain in office (unless he or she dies, resigns or becomes disqualified to be a member) until the next annual meeting of the council.[42]

The Act permits a committee to regulate the procedures to be observed at meetings and the business to be transacted at its meetings.[43]

16. Filling Casual Vacancies

Provisions of a similar nature to those of Vocational Education Committees exist in relation to filling casual vacancies. Whenever a casual vacancy occurs in a committee resulting from death, resignation or disqualification of a member, the council must appoint a replacement. A person so appointed shall stay in office for the duration of the period his or her predecessor would have remained.[44]

The person appointed to fill a casual vacancy arising from the death, resignation or disqualification of a member nominated by a voluntary rural organisation[45] shall be appointed by the same voluntary rural organisation.[46]

---

[41] The 1931 Act, s.17.

[42] *ibid.*, Sched.2, s.6.

[43] *ibid.*, s.16(4).

[44] The 1931 Act, Sched. 2, r.9, as amended by s.26(1)(e) of the 1979 Act.

[45] The 1931 Act, Sched. 2, r.2(2), as substituted by s.26(1)(a) of the 1979 Act..

[46] *ibid.*, r.9(3), inserted by s.26(1)(e) of the 1979 Act.

18. Health Board Meetings

Seven health boards were established by the Minister for Health to facilitate the administration of health services in the State, pursuant to the Health Act 1970. Each health board has a chief executive officer.

Local authorities were responsible for a number of functions now performed by health boards. Schedule 2 to the Health Act 1970 lays down the guiding principles regarding meetings of health boards.

1. Membership

Membership of the health board consists of the following categories of persons:

1. persons appointed by the applicable local authorities. The persons appointed by the relevant local authorities shall exceed the total number of other members of the health board;[1]

2. persons elected by registered medical practitioners and other designated healthcare professionals; and

3. the Minister for Health ("The Minister"), may also appoint members.

The rules governing the appointment of members to health boards are designated in Schedule 2 to the Health Act 1970.

The members of the board to be appointed by the relevant county councils shall be appointed after the annual meeting in a quinquennial year. Where members are appointed by the corporation of a county borough they shall be appointed at the quarterly meeting of the city council held in a quinquennial year. This rule is similar to the rule applicable to Dún Laoghaire borough.

The process governing the appointments by county councils,

---

[1] Health Act 1970, s.4(2)(a) and (b).

borough councils and Dún Laoghaire borough is set out in rule 3(2)(i) of Schedule 2 to the Health Act 1970.

2.   Quorum

The requirements regarding a quorum are set out in rule 15 of Schedule 2 to the Health Act 1970, which states that it shall be:

"(a) where the total number of the members of the board is a number divisible by four without a remainder—

    (i)   one-fourth of the total number of the members of the board, or

    (ii)   five,

    whichever is the greater, and

(b) Where the total number of the members of the board is a number which is not divisible by four without a remainder —

    (i)   one-fourth of the next higher number which is divisible by four without a remainder, or

    (ii)   five,

    whichever is the greater."

3.   Date of Meetings

The first meeting of the health boards shall be held on a date specified by the Minister pursuant to rule 16(1) of Schedule 2 to the 1970 Act.

A meeting of the board shall be held after each appointment of members by the relevant local authorities on a day to be appointed by the Minister. The board shall hold at least 12 meetings in each year and other meetings as are necessary.[2]

---

[2] Health Act 1970, Sched.2, r.16.

4. Chairperson and Vice-Chairperson

The board shall elect one of their members to be chairperson and likewise a vice-chairperson. That person shall remain chairperson unless he or she ceases to be, or becomes disqualified as, a member of the board, or resigns. The chairperson's term may be terminated when the board passes a resolution, for which not less than two-thirds of the members of the board voted and of which not less than seven days of notice is given to every member of the board. A similar provision applies to terminating the term of a vice-chairperson.

A chairperson or vice-chairperson may resign at any time by giving written notice of this to the board, but the resignation will not be effective until the commencement of the next meeting after the date on which the resignation was tendered.

On the election of a chairperson and vice-chairperson, where there is an equality of votes for two or more persons, the matter shall be decided by lot.

5. Proceedings at Meetings

The proceedings of a board are not invalidated by any vacancy in the membership or a defect in the appointment or disqualification of a member.[3] The chairperson calls the meeting and in his or her absence the responsibility fall to the vice-chairperson.[4] However, if the chairperson and vice-chairperson are not present, the members of the board shall choose one of their own to be chairperson.[5]

If the chairperson or in his or her absence the vice-chairperson refuses to call a meeting which has been requisitioned and where the requisition is signed by three members of the board, any three members may call a meeting. It is also provided that if the chairperson or vice-chairperson fails in response to the requisition within seven days after it was presented to him or her to call a meeting of the board, then any three members can call a meeting of the board.

There are also provisions in the 1970 Act governing the right of the Chief Executive Officer to attend meetings.

[3] Health Act 1970, Sched.2, r.18.
[4] *ibid.*, r.19.
[5] *ibid.*, r.20.

6.   Notice of Board Meetings

Three clear days of notice shall be given of the time and place of any meeting signed by the chairperson or vice-chairperson or, if called by the members, shall be fixed at the place where the board is accustomed to meet and shall specify the business to be dealt with.

Notice shall be given three days before a meeting, stating the business to be dealt with and signed by the secretary, and can be left or delivered by post to the address of every member. A failure to leave or deliver such summons shall not affect the validity of the meeting.[6]

7.   Majority and Equality of Votes

All questions shall be decided by the majority present who vote at the meeting of the board.[7] In the case of an equality of votes on any matter, the chairperson shall have a second or casting vote, except on the election of a chairperson or vice-chairperson.[8]

8.   Minutes of the Proceedings

The minutes of board meetings shall be drawn up and entered in a book kept for the purpose signed by the chairperson at that meeting or the next meeting.[9] The names of the members present shall be recorded, together with the names of members voting for and against the question before the board.[10]

9.   Interest

A member of a board who has any interest in a contract being discussed by the board must disclose the interest and its nature and shall play no

---

[6] Health Act 1970, Sched. 2, r.22.

[7] *ibid.*, r.28.

[8] *ibid.*, r.29.

[9] *ibid.*, r.25.

[10] *ibid.*, r.26.

part in the deliberation or decision on the matter. The disclosure will be recorded in the minute book.[11]

10. Casual Vacancies

A casual vacancy shall be filled by the council or corporation by whom the member causing the vacancy was appointed in the first instance within one month. A casual vacancy occurring among the other elected members shall be filled by the Minister.

11. Standing Orders

The boards may make standing orders to regulate their proceedings but these are subject to the pertinent Acts and regulations.

---

[11] Health Act 1970,.Sched.2, r.30.

Part Five: Houses of the Oireachtas

19. Meetings of the Dáil and Seanad

Article 15 of the 1937 Constitution governs the rules, procedures and privileges of the Houses of the Oireachtas. This Article gives general guidelines as to the conduct and constitution of meetings of the Dáil and Seanad.

Article 15.9.10 states that both Houses of the Oireachtas may elect their own chairperson and deputy chairperson and shall prescribe their powers and duties. However, under Article 15.10 it is provided that:

> "Each House shall make its own rules and standing orders, with power to attach penalties for their infringement, and shall have power to ensure freedom of debate, to protect its official documents and the private papers of its members, and to protect itself and its members against any person or persons interfering with, molesting or attempting to corrupt its members in the exercise of their duties."

Other provisions provide for majority voting, and for the exercise of a casting vote by the chairperson where an equality of votes occurs, *i.e.* if there is an even number of votes cast for and against a particular motion.

It is also provided that all official reports and publications of the Oireachtas and utterances made in either House shall be privileged under Article 15.13. This article guarantees parliamentary freedom and underpins the democratic process.

The Houses of the Oireachtas, under Article 15.10, have introduced standing orders concerning meetings and procedures. These standing orders are clear and prescriptive in nature and have been amended and updated as circumstances required. In the case of the Dáil, since their adoption on July 21, 1926 the standing orders have been amended on over 30 occasions. The standing orders for the present Seanad were adopted on

April 27, 1938 and have been amended nine times in total.[1]

1. The Dáil

The standing orders of the Dáil cover diverse matters. The opening of proceedings is dealt with in the early sections of the standing orders. They govern procedure on the commencement of a newly elected Dáil. Standing orders 5 to 17 detail the office of Ceann Comhairle and Leas-Cheann Comhairle.[2] There is provision for the use of the Irish and English language at standing order 18. Most Deputies conduct their Dáil and committee business through the medium of English. However, it must be understood that Irish is the first offical language and English the second, pursuant to Article 8 of the Constitution.

There are provisions regarding quorums for meetings of the Dáil, the order papers and business of the day, as well as questions to be put and rules of debate and divisions. There are further provisions detailing general committee procedures. There are specific standing orders governing access to meetings of the Dáil by the press and the public.[3]

The rules of debate are detailed in standing orders 44 to 63 and in particular refer to matters *sub judice* (restricting matters which are the subject-matter of judicial proceedings). However, this privilege is circumscribed and subject to sanction as set out in standing order 58,[4] which provides for the procedure to be adhered to where a defamatory utterance has been made by a member.

Other provisions refer generally to the office of the clerk and records of the Dáil, private members' business and the passing of Bills.

---

[1] The most recently amended standing orders relate to the Dáil and were adopted on April 29, 1997. See also the supplement to the 1977 standing orders relating to procedures and committees which came into effect on November 13, 1997. The Seanad's current standing orders were adopted on July 7, 1994.

[2] Standing order adopted April 30, 1977.

[3] See standing orders 93 and 94. Standing order 94 incorporates the provisions in Article 15.8 of the 1937 Constitution which govern the exclusion of the press and members of the public in the case of a special emergency.

[4] 1997 standing orders.

2. The Seanad

The standing orders of the Seanad are similar in nature and function to those adopted in respect of the Dáil. This is reflected in the following diverse orders. The commencement of a newly elected Seanad and the office of the Cathaoirleach and Leas-Chathaoirleach, quorum and rules of debate, divisions and the procedure on Bills are all covered. However, it should be noted that there is an absence of a specific *sub judice* rule or rules governing defamatory utterances within its standing orders, although these rules in principle do apply to the Seanad.

3. The Enforcement of Rules of Procedure in the Dáil and Seanad

It would appear that this function lies in the exclusive domain of the Dáil and Seanad.[5] Article 15.10 provides each House with power to deal with infringement of their respective standing orders and procedures.

How far these standing orders can be used as a sanction against a member who makes defamatory utterances in either House is uncertain because of the reluctance of the courts to interfere with the procedures of the Houses.[6]

A matter which has been litigated at common law and under the Constitution has the same privileges attaching to defamatory utterances made in parliament. As stated earlier this privilege is enshrined in the standing orders of the two Houses.

---

[5] See *Wireless Dealers Association v. Fair Trade Commission*, unreported, Supreme Court, March 14, 1956. It was held that the courts have no jurisdiction to interfere with the introduction of a Bill into the Seanad, which the applicants claimed was unconstitutional. This decision indicates the clear recognition given by the courts to the separation of powers doctrine. This issue was raised more recently in an application for leave to apply for a judicial review of the suspension of a senator made by the Cathaoirleach of the Seanad; see the *Irish Times*, March 8, 1990.

[6] 1997 standing orders for the Dáil and the 1994 standing orders for the Senate. See also the decision in the English case of *Dillon v. Balfour* [1887] 20 L.R. Ir. 600, where it was held that: "Statements made by members of either House of Parliament in their places in the House, though they might be untrue to their knowledge could not be made the foundation of civil or criminal proceedings however injurious they might be to the interests of a third party". This principle has its origin in the Bill of Rights 1688 (1 Will. & Mar. sess. 2, c. 2).

In *O'Malley v. An Ceann Cómhairle*,[7] the applicant, who was a member of Dáil Éireann had tabled a question in the Dáil to be answered by the Minister for Enterprise and Employment on May 24, 1989. On May 23, 1989 the Ceann Comhairle wrote to the applicant saying that he was disallowing part of the question as it would involve repetition in light of answers already received from the Minister.

Because of this refusal by the Ceann Comhairle to allow the question to stand unamended, the Dáil member sought leave to judicially review the order on the grounds that it was in breach of order 3 of the standing orders of the Dáil.

In the High Court Barron J. refused the applicant leave to apply by way of judicial review, holding that judicial review proceedings were not appropriate as this was an internal matter for Dáil Éireann for which there was an internal means of review.

The applicant appealed to the Supreme Court. Dismissing the appeal, O'Flaherty J. stated:

> "How questions should be framed for answer by Ministers of the Government is so much a matter concerning the internal working of Dáil Éireann that it would seem to be inappropriate for the court to intervene except in some very extreme circumstances which it is impossible to envisage at the moment. But, further, it involves to such a degree the operation of the internal machinery of debate in the house as to remain within the competence of Dáil Éireann to deal with exclusively, having regard to Article 5, s. 10 of the Constitution."[8]

4. Absolute Privilege for Utterances in the Dáil and Seanad

Privilege may be absolute or qualified. In the case of a member of the Oireachtas, he or she has absolute privilege pursuant to Articles 15.12 and 15.13 of the constitution in respect of all utterances made in either House wherever published.

In *Attorney General v. Hamilton (No. 2)*, Geoghegan J. stated

---

[7] [1997] 1 I.R. 427.
[8] *ibid.*, at 431.

inter alia that "legislators are free to represent the interests of their constituents without fear that they will be later called to task in the Courts for that representation..."⁹

There is statutory recognition of absolute privilege arising out of utterances made during the legislative process whether in committee or on the floor of either House during debates in the Defamation Act 1961. The Committees of the Houses of the Oireachtas (Privilege and Procedure) Act 1976 was enacted to clarify the existence of this absolute privilege in relation to utterances made in or before a committee of either House.

5.   Privilege from Arrest and Obstruction

It would appear that members of the Dáil and Seanad are entitled to be protected against arrest and other obstruction when travelling to meetings of the Oireachtas.

This matter came into public focus in a recent case involving possible proceedings against a senator travelling from the Seanad to his home. A prosecution arising out of an alleged drink driving offence was not proceeded with after the senator was alleged to have invoked the constitutional privilege of Article 15.13 which states:

> "The members of each House of the Oireachtas shall, except in case of treason as defined in this Constitution, felony or breach of the peace, be privileged from arrest in going to and returning from, and while within the precincts of, either House, and shall not, in respect of any utterance in either House, be amenable to any court or any authority other than the House itself."

---

⁹ [1993] 3 I.R. 227.

Part Six: Company Meetings and Procedures

20. Annual General Meetings

The annual general meeting (AGM) provides the members of a company with an opportunity to familiarise themselves with the financial state of the company. It also enables them to request information from the directors on how the affairs of the company have been conducted in the previous year and to exert pressure on the directors if the company is not operating satisfactorily.

Every company must in each year hold an AGM in addition to any other meetings held in that year,[1] meaning the calendar year.[2]

The notice convening the meeting shall specify that it is an AGM.[3] Not more than 15 months shall elapse between the date of one AGM of the company and that of the next.[4] The first AGM of the company need not be held in the year of incorporation or in the following year so long as it is held within 18 months of incorporation.[5]

Lush J., in *Gibson v. Barton*, interpreting a similar section in the English Companies Act, held that:

"The construction of the statute is perfectly plain in the first calendar year of the registration of a company they are not bound to hold a general meeting if there are not six months in that year in which to hold the first general meeting, but all subsequent meetings are to be held once in every calendar year".[6]

If a company has defaulted in the holding of an AGM the Minister may, on the application of a member of the company, call or direct the calling of an AGM and give such directions as he or she believes fit and necessary.[7] The Minister can direct that one member of the company present,

---

[1] Companies Act 1963, s.131(1).
[2] *Gibson v. Barton* (1875) LR 10 Q.B. 329, *per* Lush J.
[3] Companies Act 1963, s.131(1).
[4] *ibid.*
[5] *ibid.*, s.131(2).
[6] Above, n.2.
[7] Companies Act 1963, s.131(3).

in person or by proxy, shall be deemed to constitute a meeting.[8] A general meeting held pursuant to the Minister's order will be treated as an AGM, but if such meeting is not held in the year when the default in holding it occurred, it may be treated as an AGM for the year in which it was actually held if the company resolves that this be so.[9] If the company resolves such a meeting be treated as an AGM, a copy of the resolution to this effect must be forwarded to the Registrar of Companies within 15 days.[10] If the situation occurs where a company, having resolved that a particular meeting be treated as an AGM, fails to forward a copy of this resolution within 15 days to the Registrar of Companies, it shall be liable to a fine of £100.[11]

If there is default in holding a meeting,[12] or in complying with a direction of the Minister, the company and every officer in default shall be liable to a fine not exceeding £500.

The first AGM shall be held in the State.[13] In other years it may be held outside the State if the articles provide or members resolve in writing it be held elsewhere.[14]

If it is impractical to call or convene the meeting in the manner as provided in the articles, the court may, of its own motion or on the application of a director or a member entitled to vote at the meeting, make an order that such a meeting be held and give such direction as it sees fit in regard to such a meeting, including that one member present, in person or by proxy, shall be deemed to constitute a meeting.[15]

Such a meeting shall be considered a meeting duly called, held and conducted.[16] The sole member of a single-member company may decide to dispense with the holding of an AGM and if this happens, then the provisions of section 131 of the Companies Act 1963 shall not apply to such a company.

---

[8] Companies Act 1963, s.131(3).

[9] *ibid.*, s.131(4).

[10] *ibid.*, s.131(5).

[11] *ibid.*, s.131(6).

[12] *ibid.*, s.131(1).

[13] *ibid.*, First Schedule, Table A, reg. 47.

[14] *Shannonside Holding*, unreported, High Court, Costello J., May 20, 1993; see also the Companies Act 1963, s.140 (1A) and (1B).

[15] *ibid.*, s.13(1).

[16] *ibid.*, s.135(2).

Recognition was given to single member companies pursuant to the European Community (Single Member Private Limited Companies) Regulations 1994.[16a] If the sole member or company auditor calls an AGM, however, by giving notice to the company not less than three months before the end of the year, when such notice is given the provisions of section 131 of the 1963 Act should apply with respect to the calling of the meeting and in consequence of default.

1. Presiding at an Annual General Meeting

If the articles of association contain no provisions for the appointment of a chairpeson for such a meeting, then section 134, subsection D of the Companies Act 1963 shall apply to this situation by providing that any member elected by the meeting may be chairperson.

The chairperson, if any, of the board of directors shall preside at every AGM of the company and if there is no such chairperson or if he is not present within 15 minutes after the time appointed for the holding of the meeting, the directors present shall elect one of their members to be chairperson.[17]

2. Notice of an Annual General Meeting

Every notice convening an AGM must identify the meeting as being an AGM.[18] The notice must fairly disclose the business of the meeting and must be frank, open and free from ambiguity and written in language understood by ordinary people.[19]

The people who are entitled to receive notice of an Annual General Meeting are:

1. Every member of the company.

[16a] European Communities (Single-Member Private Limited Companies) Regulations 1994, S.I. No. 275 of 1994.

[17] Companies Act 1963, Table A, art. 13.

[18] *ibid.*, s.131(1).

[19] *Faye v. Croyden Tramways Company* (1898) ICH 358.

2. A personal representative of a deceased shareholder. Such a representative is recognised as having title to the deceased member's share interest pursuant to regulation 29 (Part I of Table A). However, prior to being registered as a member in respect of a share, the representative is not entitled to exercise any right conferred by membership in regard to a meeting of the company.[20]

3. The official assignee in bankruptcy if a member is bankrupt.

4. The auditor of the company must receive notice[21] and, in the case of an auditor,[22] the notice must be served in the manner prescribed by Table A of the Companies Act 1963. A notice may be given by the company to any member either personally or by sending it by post to his or her registered address.[23]

The accidental omission to give notice of a meeting, or the non-receipt of notices of a meeting by any person entitled to receive notice shall not invalidate the proceedings at the meeting,[24] but a deliberate failure to give notice to a person entitled to receive notice will render the meeting invalid.

In this regard a failure by directors of a company to give members notice of an AGM, because they were under the erroneous impression that the member, having executed transfers of the shares, was no longer a member of the company and so was not entitled to notice of the meeting in question, was held to be invalid.[25]

A company may be restrained from holding an AGM where the notice convening it and the accompanying circular are inaccurate or misleading.

In a case involving a proposal to alter the articles of association by authorising advances to directors on their personal security, the court

---

[20] See the Companies Act 1963, Table A, Pt. 1, reg 32; see also *Arulchelvan v. Wright*, unreported, High Court, July 20, 1996.

[21] *ibid.*, Table A, art. 136.

[22] Companies Act 1990, s.193.

[23] Companies Act 1963, Table A, Pt.1, art. 133.

[24] *ibid.*, Pt.11, art. 9.

[25] *Musselwhite v. CH. Musselwhite & Son Ltd* [1962] 2 Ch. 964.

found that the circular which accompanied the notice might mislead the shareholders; the statements contained in it were calculated to have the effect of obtaining proxies from shareholders without providing them with the information which would enable them to form a correct judgment as to who were the proper persons to whom votes could be entrusted.[26]

In order that a special resolution may be valid under section 141(2) of the Companies Act 1948 (similar to the equivalent provision in the Companies Act 1963), the notice has to specify the entire text, or the entire substance of the resolution which is intended to be proposed as a special resolution; the resolution as passed should be the same resolution as that identified in the notice circulated to members (though grammatical or clerical errors may be corrected provided these are no departure from the substance of the proposed resolution).[27]

3. Quorum

In the case of a private company, two members, and in the case of other companies, three members, present in person shall constitute a quorum.[28] There are exceptions to this rule where the Minister, pursuant to section 131, or the courts pursuant to section 135, in directing that a meeting be held may direct that one member of the company constitute a quorum.

No business shall be transacted at any AGM unless a quorum of members is achieved at the time the meeting proceeds to business.[29] The quorum must be maintained throughout the meeting.[30]

At the AGM there is a mandatory requirement that a profit and loss account, a balance sheet, the auditor's report,[31] and the necessary directors' report[32] on the state of the company be presented to the meeting. The profit and loss account must cover the period from the previous accounts to a date not earlier than nine months before the meeting, or in the case of a first meeting, from the date of incorporation.[33] The balance

---

[26] *Jackson v. Munster Bank Limited* [1884] 13 L.R. Ir. 118.

[27] *Moorgate Mercantile Holdings* [1980] 1 W.L.R. 227.

[28] Companies Act 1963, s.131(3).

[29] *ibid.*, s.140(1).

[30] *Re London Flats* [1969] 1 W.L.R. 711.

[31] Companies Act 1963, s.163.

[32] *ibid.*, s.158.

[33] *ibid.*, s.148.

sheet must be as of the date up to which the profit and loss account is made up.[34]

It is an essential prerequisite of an AGM that a copy of the balance sheet, profit and loss account, auditor's report and the directors' report be sent to every member of the company and every debenture holder and all persons who are entitled to receive notice of the AGM at least 21 days before the meeting.[35]

Other business to be dealt with at the AGM includes the appointment of, or reappointment of, the auditor and the fixing of his remuneration;[36] declaration of a dividend; the consideration of the accounts; and the election of directors in place of any retiring.[37]

In the case of a single member company the provisions of section 148 of the 1963 Act are satisfied where such accounts and reports are sent to the sole member, not less than 21 days before the date of the meeting.[38]

At the AGM of the company the auditor's report shall be read out and shall be available for inspection to any member.[39]

The auditor, if qualified, is automatically re-appointed unless a resolution is passed at the meeting appointing someone else, or if such a resolution provides that he or she should not be re-appointed (in such instance special notice of the resolution is required), or if the auditor has given notice in writing of his or her unwillingness to be re-appointed.[40]

There is no requirement that the AGM approves or adopts the accounts and reports of the company. Every balance sheet and profit and loss account of a company shall be signed on behalf of the directors by two of the company's directors.[41]

The profit and loss account, if it is not incorporated in the balance sheet or any group accounts laid before the AGM of a company shall be annexed to the balance sheet and the auditor's report shall be attached to it. The accounts so annexed shall be approved by the board of directors

---

[34] Companies Act 1963, s.148(2).

[35] *ibid.*, s.159(1).

[36] *ibid.*, s.160.

[37] *ibid.*, Table A, art.53.

[38] S.I. No. 275 of 1994, reg.8(9).

[39] Companies Act 1963, s.193(2).

[40] *ibid.*, s.160(2).

[41] *ibid.*, s.156(2).

prior to the balance sheet and profit and loss account being signed.[42]

There are special provisions to be dealt with in regard to the appointment of directors at an AGM.

No person, other than a retiring director or a person recommended by a director, shall be eligible for election unless a notice signed by a member entitled to vote at such a meeting and a notice signed by that person stating his or her willingness to act as a director are left at the company's registered office between the third and twenty-first days before the meeting.[43]

A motion for the appointment of two or more persons as directors of the company by a single resolution shall not be made unless a resolution that it be made has been agreed in the first instance by the meeting without any vote being given for or against it.[44]

4.   Minutes of the Meeting

Every company shall, as soon as possible, enter the minutes of all proceedings into a book for that purpose; where such minutes are signed by the chairperson at that meeting or at the next meeting, they shall be evidence of such proceedings.[45]

The minutes shall be kept in bound books or recordings of the matter kept by another method. Section 4 of the Companies (Amendment) Act 1977 allows for the keeping of computerised records.

The minutes shall be kept at the registered office of the company and be available for inspection for two hours each day by the members of the company on payment of an inspection fee.[46]

---

[42] Companies Act 1963, s.157(1).

[43] *ibid.*, Table A, art.96.

[44] *ibid.*, s.181; see *Moylan v. Irish Whiting Manufacturers*, unreported, High Court, April 14th, 1980.

[45] Companies Act 1963, s.145.

[46] *ibid.*, s.146.

21. Extraordinary General Meetings

All general meetings other than annual general meetings are called extra-ordinary general meetings (EGMs).[1] The authority to convene an EGM lies with the board of directors as can be seen from article 50 of Table A of the Companies Act 1963.

1. Convening an EGM

If the directors of a company fail to hold a meeting, the board may, on the requisition of members holding not less than one tenth of the paid-up capital as carries a right of voting at general meetings of the company, call an extraordinary general meeting. If a company does not have a share capital, then members representing at least one tenth of the total voting rights with the right to vote at general meetings may convene an extraordinary general meeting.[2]

The requisitionists must state the objects of the meeting and these must be filed in the registered office.[3] Section 132(2) of the 1963 Act provides that if the directors do not, within 21 days from the date of the deposit of the requisition, proceed to convene a meeting to be held within two months of that date, the requisitionists or any of them representing more than one half of the total voting rights may themselves convene a meeting; that meeting must be held within three months from that date.

The court has inherent power under section 135 of the 1963 Act to direct the calling of a meeting where the company is unable to do so. It may do this on its own motion resulting from an application made by a director or member entitled to vote. Where the court makes such an order, it shall direct how proceedings are to be conducted and may also provide that one member present, in person or by proxy, shall constitute a quorum.[4]

---

[1] Companies Act 1963, First Schedule, Table A, reg.9.

[2] *ibid.*, s.132(1).

[3] *ibid.*, s.132(2); see also First Schedule, Table A, reg.50.

[4] *ibid.*, s.135(1).

If at any time there are not within the State sufficient directors to form a quorum, any director or two members may convene an EGM.

Where an auditor wishes to give an explanation in connection with his or her resignation, he or she may requisition a meeting for this and every member is entitled to a copy of the auditor's notice of explanation. In any notice calling such a meeting there shall be incorporated an auditor's statement regarding the circumstances of his or her resignation which shall be served on every member of the company with the notice convening the meeting.

All general meetings of the company which has adopted Table A of the 1963 Act shall be held in the State unless the members resolve that it should be held outside the State.[5]

2. Notice of EGMs

Ordinarily an EGM requires not less than 14 days of notice in writing.[6] However, the following exceptions to this rule apply:

1. 21 days of notice in writing for the passing of a special resolution;[7]
2. seven days of notice is required in the case of an unlimited company.

The notice convening an EGM is issued by the secretary, subject to the authority of the directors.[8] If a secretary exceeds his or her authority and issues a notice in excess of such authority, the board may subsequently ratify the notice prior to the meeting.[9] A notice must be certain and free from ambiguity.[10]

A notice may be served on any member, either personally or by post, at his or her registered address and if it is sent by post, service of the notice shall be deemed to be effected by addressing, pre-paying and post-

---

5 For further analysis see *Re Shannonside Holdings*, unreported, High Court, Costello J., May 20, 1993.

6 Companies Act 1963, s.133(1)(a), (b).

7 A resolution shall be a special resolution when it has been passed by not less than three quarters of the votes cast by such members and it requires 21 days of notice in writing: *ibid.*, s.141(1).

8 See below, n.14; see also *Re Brick and Stone Co.* [1878] W.&N. 140.

9 *Hooper v. Kerr* [1900] 83 L.T. 72.

10 *Kaye v. Croyden Tramways Company* [1898] 1 Ch. 358.

ing a letter containing the notice so as to have been effected at the expiration of 24 hours after the letter is posted.

A notice may be given by the company to the joint holders of a share by giving the notice to the joint holder first named in the register.[11] A notice may be given to persons entitled to a share in consequence of death[12] or bankruptcy of a member.[13]

Notice of an EGM shall be given to every member or every person upon whom the ownership of a share devolves as a result of his or her being the personal representative or the official assignee in bankruptcy of a member who but for his death or bankruptcy would have been entitled to receive notice.[14] The auditor shall be entitled to receive notice of all general meetings, including EGMs.[15]

---

[11] Companies Act 1963, First Schedule, Table A, reg. 134.

[12] The personal representative has to be registered as a member: *Arulchelvan v. Wright*, unreported, High Court, July 20, 1996.

[13] Companies Act 1963, First Schedule, Table A, reg. 135.

[14] *ibid.*, reg. 136.

[15] *ibid.*

22. Class Meetings

A company may have a share capital which is divided into different classes of shares. However, a company may decide to vary the rights attaching to such shares. In those circumstances it may be necessary to hold a meeting or meetings of the class or classes affected. Section 38 of the Companies (Amendment) Act 1983 contains provisions regarding variations of class rights of shareholders.

The provisions contained in sections 133 and 134 of the Companies Act 1963 apply to class meetings unless the company's articles of association do not contain other provisions to the contrary.

The Companies (Amendment) Act 1983 adds a further provision, namely:

"(a)   the necessary quorum at any such meeting other than an adjourned meeting shall be two persons holding or representing by proxy at least one-third in nominal value of the issued shares of the class in question and at an adjourned meeting one person holding shares of the class in question or his proxy."[1]

It is also provided that the quorum for an adjourned meeting shall be two persons holding shares or representing by proxy at least one third in nominal value of the issued shares of the class in question. It is further provided that in the case of an adjourned meeting one person holding shares of the class shall be a proxy.[2]

Any holder of shares of the class in question present in person or by proxy may demand a poll.[3]

1.   Meetings of Compromises and Arrangements

Where a compromise or arrangement is proposed between a company and

---

[1] Companies (Amendment) Act 1983, s.38(6)(a).

[2] *ibid.*.

[3] *ibid.*, s.38(6)(b).

its creditors or any class of them, or between the company and its members or any class of them, the court may, on the application of the company (or the creditors, the members, or a liquidator if the company is being wound up), order a meeting of the creditors or a class of them or members or class of members, as the case may be, to be summoned in whatever manner the court directs.[4]

If the majority in number representing three quarters in value of the creditors or class of creditors or members present and voting, either in person or by proxy, at a meeting vote in favour of a resolution agreeing to any compromise or arrangement, the compromise or arrangement shall if sanctioned by the court be binding on all the creditors or class of creditors or the members or class of members, as the case may be, and also on the company and, in the case of a company being wound up, on the liquidator and contributories of the company.[5]

The company must decide what class or classes will be affected by such an arrangement or compromise. It will be necessary to organise separate meetings of each class of members and creditors.

In the case of *Sovereign Life Assurance Company v. Dodd* the term "class" was defined as follows:

> "It seems that one must give a meaning to the term class as will prevent the section being so worked, as to result in confiscation and injustice and that it must be confined to those persons whose rights are not so dissimilar as to make it impossible for them to consult together with a view to their common interest."[6]

Every notice summoning a meeting under section 201(1) of the Companies Act 1963 must have attached to it a statement explaining the effect of the compromise and in particular stating any material interest of

---

[4] Companies Act 1963, s.201. See also the case of *Re Pye (Ireland) Limited*, Unreported, Costello J. November 12, 1984 where it was held that a second application should not be entertained except in exceptional circumstances.

[5] Companies Act 1963, s.201(3).

[6] *Sovereign Life Assurance Company v. Dodd* [1892] 2 Q.B.573. See also comments of Costello J. in *Re Pye (Ireland) Limited*, referring to class meetings, *ibid.*: "It is for the company to decide which group should be treated as separate classes, however, if the correct meetings are not held the Court may not sanction the scheme. Unsecured creditors will normally form a single class except where some are to be treated differently and have different interests from the rest".

the directors of the company whether as directors, or as members or creditors of the company.

In every notice summoning a meeting, which is given by advertisement, there must be included such a statement or notification to the members attending the meeting where copies of such a statement may be obtained.[7] Where the compromises or arrangements affect the rights of debenture holders of the company, the statement shall give a similar explanation in relation to the trustees of any deed for securing the issue of a debenture as required to give in relation to the company directors.[8] The provisions contained in section 202 of the Companies Act 1963 must be complied with in regard to any notice which issues and the statements explaining the effect of the arrangement on the directors and debenture holders. In *City Property Investment Trust Corporation*, petitioners' demands for separate meetings of different classes of shareholders were authorised by the court to consider a scheme of arrangement and the sending of notices by post and the giving of notice by way of advertisement.[9] The advertisement had stated where the scheme could be seen but it did not refer in any way to the explanatory statement accompanying it and because of the omission the meeting was held to be invalid.

The summons must be supported by a grounding affidavit outlining the proposed scheme and giving the names and addresses of the chairperson and vice-chairperson of the meeting.

If the court makes an order allowing the application, it will direct that the company should convene a meeting and issue a notice to every person entitled to notice. The advertisement should appear in *Iris Oifigiúil*.

The notice must be accompanied by copies of the scheme of arrangement, proxy forms and voting cards.

The articles of the company may specify the type of proxy to be used and this must be strictly adhered to. If the compromise or arrangement is sanctioned by the court, it is binding on all the members or class of members, or creditors or class of them, or if the company is being wound up, the liquidator and contributories of the company.

---

[7] Companies Act 1963, s.202(1)(b).

[8] *ibid.*, s.202(2).

[9] 1951 S.L.T. 871.

23. Directors' Meetings

The functions of the directors are to manage the company and to exercise their powers in accordance with the provisions of the Companies Acts, directions given to them by the company in a general meeting, and company regulations.

In managing the affairs of the company the directors' overriding concern must be to always act in the best interest of the company.

1. Directors' Meetings

The directors may meet together to despatch their business and regulate their meetings as they think fit; it follows that a director may, and the secretary shall on the requisition of a director, summon a meeting of the directors. The directors must act collectively in the exercise of their duties.

2. Notice

Notice of a directors' meeting must be given to all directors resident in the State and failure to do so many render the meeting invalid.

This principle was dealt with in the case of *Portuguese Consolidated Copper Mines Ltd*[1] where it was held that a director could not waive his right to notice as he was within reach and it was perfectly possible to give him notice of the meeting. "The circumstances existing at the time when he used the words relied on as a waiver might have been wholly altered or he might have taken a different view if had notice of the time and object of the meeting. That notice ought to have been given to him."

If the directors agree that notice need not be given of the meeting, then it shall not be necessary to give notice of a meeting to a director who is outside the State.

---

[1] (1889) 42 Ch. D. 160 at 168.

The law does not stipulate any defined period as being required for a notice convening a board meeting to specify the business which is to be transacted.

An unreasonable period of notice will be deemed to be invalid. This matter was dealt with in the case of *Re Homer District Consolidated Gold Mines*[2] where two directors out of a total of four held a meeting of which very short notice was given to the other directors of the company. The notice of the meeting, which was to be held at 2 p.m., was posted at 11 a.m. on the same day. It was held by the court on the evidence tendered regarding the notice in question that the two directors present knew that one of the other two summoned could not be present until 3 p.m. and they did not know if the other director could come to the meeting. Their decision to rescind a resolution passed at a previous meeting was held to be invalid.

A resolution in writing signed by all the directors who were entitled to receive notice of a directors' meeting shall be as valid as if it had been passed at a meeting of the directors duly convened and held.

3. Chairperson

The directors elect the chairperson of the meeting and may determine the period for which he or she is to hold office. If the power of electing a chairperson has been delegated by the company to the directors, it cannot then be controlled or affected by the company unless the contract is altered by special resolution.

The election of a chairperson of directors made in contravention of the Articles of Association is void and cannot be regularised by mere acquiescence.

4. Presiding at a Directors' Meeting

It is usually the elected chairperson who presides at a meeting of the directors but if the directors have failed to elect such a person, or if the elected individual is not present within five minutes after the time appointed for holding the meeting, the directors may choose one of their number to be chairperson of the meeting The chairperson may be

---

[2] (1888) 39 Ch. D. 546.

removed by the directors at any time.

5. Quorum

The quorum necessary for transaction of business by the directors may be fixed by them and, unless so fixed, it shall be two members.

In *Boron v. Potter*[3] of a meeting where two directors met accidentally without notice and one of them proceeded to call a directors' meeting against the wishes of the other, the meeting was held to be invalid.

If a vacancy exists reducing the number of directors to less than that specified as required in the regulations, the only business that the directors can undertake is to increase the number of directors to the appropriate quorum level or to summon a general meeting.

A director may be disqualified from forming part of a quorum or from voting on any contract or arrangement in which he has an interest.

6. Minutes

Minute books must be kept, recording the names of all directors present at such meetings and all the proceedings and resolutions. The minutes should record the names of the directors arriving late or leaving the meeting early.

Minutes must be kept which record the proceedings of the meetings of the directors' committees. The minutes of directors' meetings and of their committees must be entered in the minute book as soon as possible.

Any minute recorded in accordance with section 145(1) of the Companies Act 1963 and signed by the chairman of that meeting or of the next meeting shall be evidence of the proceedings of that meeting.

Where the minutes have been recorded in accordance with section 145, then the meeting at which such minutes have been made shall be held to have been properly convened and the proceedings at such meeting held to be valid until the contrary is proven.

The minutes of directors' meetings may be drafted in advance in the case of a small company meeting only when an actual decision is required. The decision in such circumstances will usually have been reached in advance of the meeting; therefore the directors will simply

---

[3] [1914] 1 Ch. 895.

confirm what has already been agreed.

7.   Resolutions

Sectin 144 of the Companies Act 1963 states that where a resolution is passed at an adjourned meeting of the directors it shall be deemed to have been passed on the date on which it was in fact passed.

Where a resolution is passed at a directors' meeting that an old public limited company be re-registered as a public limited company, a copy of this shall be registered with the Registrar of Companies. It is also provided that where a resolution is passed at a directors' meeting that shares in a public limited company which have been forfeited or have been acquired by a public limited company be cancelled, a copy of the resolution shall be registered with the Registrar of Companies.

Where a resolution purports to have been passed at a board meeting, but that board meeting has not taken place, then, irrespective of whether the resolution is signed by the specified number of directors, it shall be deemed invalid.

The directors of a company may, at a board meeting where they propose to wind up the company voluntarily, make a statutory declaration that having made a full inquiry into the affairs of the company they are satisfied that the company will be able to pay its debts within 12 months of the commencement of winding up.

8.   Directors' Committees

The directors may delegate any of their powers to a committee consisting of such member or members of the board as they deem fit and may designate their terms of reference. Such a committee will be subject to any regulations imposed on it by the directors.

The committee may elect a chairperson of its meeting; if its chairperson is not present within five minutes after the time appointed for holding the meeting, the members may choose one of their members to be chairperson.

The committee may adjourn its meetings as it thinks fit. All questions at its meetings shall be decided by the majority, and if there is an equality of votes, the chairperson shall have a second or casting vote.

152

24. Meetings and Winding Up

1.   Voluntary Winding Up

A company may be wound up voluntarily in the following circumstances:

1.   Where the period fixed by the articles regarding its existence has expired; or

2.   Where the company resolves by way of special resolution that it be wound up; or

3.   Where the company resolves that it cannot by reason of its liabilities continue its business and that it be wound up voluntarily.[1]

2.   Meetings Prior to a Winding Up

The procedures for such voluntary meetings are subject to the relevant provisions in the Companies Act and the company's own articles.

Where it is proposed that a company be wound up voluntarily, the directors must hold a meeting. At the meeting the directors will make a statutory declaration that they have made an inquiry into the affairs of the company and that they are of the opinion that it will be able to pay its debts for a period not exceeding 12 months.[2]

3.   The Statutory Declaration of Solvency

This declaration must be made within 28 days preceding the date of the passing of the resolution for the winding up of the company and this shall be delivered to the Registrar of Companies in accordance with the provi-

---

[1] Companies Act 1963, s.251(1)(a), (b) and (c).
[2] *ibid.*, s.256(1).

sions of section 143 of the Companies Act 1963.[3]

The declaration must state the company's assets and liabilities at the latest date up to the date of declaration and in any event not more than three months before the declaration.[4] This report is attached to the declaration and also the notice issued by the company of the general meeting at which it is intended to propose the resolution for the members' voluntary winding up.

When the company has, at its general meeting, passed a resolution for a voluntary winding up, the resolution shall within 14 days after the passage of such resolution be published in Iris Oifigiúil.[5] The company may appoint a liquidator at its meeting.[6]

It should be noted that this extraordinary general meeting should be held within 28 days of the date of declaration of solvency, and subject to any provisions contained in the articles of the company.[7] It is to be noted that the liquidator may convene a meeting whenever he thinks it is proper to do so.

In the event of a winding up continuing for more than a year the liquidator shall summon a general meeting at the end of the first year from the commencement of the winding up and within three months after the end of each year and the liquidator must submit an account of such meeting to the Registrar of Companies.[8]

There are other situations where a members' voluntary winding may designated a creditors' voluntary winding up. If the statutory declaration of solvency is not filed the winding up will be a creditors' voluntary winding up and the directors must convene with the members an extraordinary general meeting to pass the necessary resolution that the company cannot by reason of its liabilities continue in business and it would be advisable that they wind up the company. The directors shall

---

[3] Companies Act 1963, s.256, (2) (a).

[4] Section 128 of the Companies Act 1990 amends section 256 of the 1963 Act which provides that a report on the financial state of the company has to be drawn up by some independent person, that is, a person qualified at the time to be, or to continue to be, an auditor of the company.

[5] Companies Act 1963, s.252.

[6] *ibid.*, s.258 (1).

[7] Quorums, proxies, methods of voting and procedures are regulated by the articles of association of the company and any relevant provisions in the Companies Acts.

[8] Companies Act 1963, s.262(1).

also call a meeting of the creditors to be summoned for the next day following the day on which the resolution for a voluntary winding up is to be proposed and the notice of such a creditors' meeting must be sent by post to the creditor or creditors at least 10 days before the date of the meeting.[9]

The company directors shall advertise the notice of the creditors' meeting at least 10 days before the date of the meeting once in two daily newspapers circulating in the area where the office of the company is situated.[10]

The directors of the company shall place a full statement of the company's affairs and the list of creditors before the meeting of the creditors. The directors will elect one of their fellow directors to preside at the meeting.

Where the liquidator is, at any time, of the opinion that the company will not be able to pay its debts in full within the period stipulated in the declaration, he shall summon a meeting of the creditors not later than 14 days after the day he forms such an opinion.[11]

The liquidator shall send a notice of the creditors' meeting by post not less than seven days before the day on which the meeting is to be held.[12] He shall publish a notice of the creditors' meeting 10 days before the meeting in Iris Oifigiúil and two daily newspapers circulating in the area where the company's place of business is situated.[13] The liquidator must furnish the creditors with relevant information concerning the affairs of the company free of charge, if required, before the date of the meeting.[14] He shall make out a statement in the prescribed form on the affairs of the company which should include a list of the company's assets and liabilities and a list of outstanding creditors and the amount of their claims. The liquidator must lay this before the meeting of the creditors and attend and preside at the meeting.[15]

At the creditors' meeting they may nominate a person to be a liquidator and despite the fact that the members in general meeting have nominated a different liquidator, the final choice of liquidator lies with

---

[9] Companies Act 1963, s.266(1).

[10] *ibid.*, s.266(2).

[11] *ibid.*, s.261(1)(a).

[12] *ibid.*, s.261(1)(b).

[13] *ibid.*, s.261(1)(c).

[14] *ibid.*, s.261(1)(d).

[15] *ibid.*, s.261(2).

the creditors.[16]
The creditors at their meeting may appoint a committee of inspection which shall consist of not more than five persons nominated by the creditors. Where such a committee is appointed, the members of the company may appoint three persons to act as members of the committee. These can be objected to by the creditors and unless an application is made to the court they will be disqualified from acting on the committee.

4. Final Meeting in a Voluntary Liquidation

When the affairs of a company are fully wound up, the liquidator will summon a general meeting of the company, before which he will lay his account of the winding up, showing how it has been conducted and how the property of the company has been disposed of.[17] That meeting shall be advertised in two daily newspapers circulating in the area in which the registered office is situated stating the time, place and object of the meeting and this notice must be published at least 28 days before the meeting.[18]

It is to be noted that in any creditors' voluntary winding up the liquidator may summon a meeting of the creditors at any time to ascertain their wishes.[19] The court may make the necessary order and decide on any matters of conflict arising from the meeting from creditors and contributors.

---

[16] A liquidator is appointed to wind up the affairs of the company and to realise and distribute its assets, see s.258(1) of the 1963 Act.

[17] Companies Act 1963, s.263(1).

[18] *ibid.*, s.263(2).

[19] RSC 1986, Ord. 74, r.54(2).

25. Compulsory Winding Up

A company may be wound up by the court pursuant to section 212 of the companies Act 1963 in the following circumstances.

1. Where the company has by special resolution resolved that the company be wound up by the court.

2. Where the company does not commence business within a year from its incorporation or suspends business for a whole year.

3. Where the number of members is reduced in the case of a private company below two and in other companies below seven.

4. Where the company is unable to pay its debts.

5. Where the court is of the opinion that it is just and equitable that it be wound up.

6. Where the court is satisfied that the affairs of the company are being conducted in an oppressive manner.

It should be noted that after the end of the general transitional period within the meaning of the Companies (Amendment) Act 1983, the company is an old public limited company.

1. Petition for Winding Up

An application is made to the court in these circumstances for the winding up of the company by way of petition, presented either by the company or by any creditor or creditors or contributories or by all of them together or separately.[1] The court may also appoint a liquidator pursuant to section 225 of the Companies Act 1963.

---

[1] Companies Act 1963, s.213.

2. Appointment of Committee of Inspection

Where a winding up order has been·made by the court the liquidator shall, if the court orders, summon a meeting of the company's creditors or separate meetings of the creditors or contributories to determine if an application should be made for the appointment of an inspection committee to act with the liquidator.[2]

3. Meetings of Creditors and Contributories

The court may direct that a meeting of creditors and contributories of the company to be held to ascertain the wishes of both groups in regard to the winding up under section 309 of the Companies Act 1963. The court may also appoint a person to act as chairperson and to report on the result of the meeting to the court.

The offical liquidator shall give notice in writing seven clear days before the day appointed for such meeting to every creditor or contributory of the time and place of the meeting. The purpose of this meeting is to ascertain the wishes of the creditors and contributories and this must be made known to both of these groups in advance of any meeting.[3]

The court may direct that notice of the meeting may be given by way of advertisement though the object of the meeting need not be stated.[4] Where the court appoints the chairperson of such meeting, he or she shall preside at such meeting and make a report of the result.[5]

4. Rules as to Meetings in a Compulsory Winding Up

Meetings of creditors in a creditors' voluntary winding up, and of credi-

---

[2] Companies Act 1963, s.215.

[3] RSC, Ord. 74, r.50 as amended and also s.232 of the Companies Act 1963.

[3] An official liquidator is appointed by the court pursuant to s.228(b).

[4] RSC, Ord. 74, r.55 (1).

[5] *ibid.*, Ord. 74,·r.55 (2).

tors or contributories in a compulsory winding up, must be held in accordance with the winding up rules.[6]

The following is a brief outline of the rules as set out in the Rules of the Superior Courts.

Notice

Meetings are convened by giving not less than seven days' notice by post to every creditor and contributory and forms of special or general proxy must be sent with the notice.

Place of Meeting

In the case of a company having its registered place of business in the county borough of Dublin or in the county borough of Cork, the person convening the meeting must convene it for a venue which is convenient for the majority of creditors or contributories or both. In any other case a person convening the meeting must select a venue most convenient for the majority of creditors or contributories or both. Different times or places may be named for the meetings of creditors and meetings of contributories.

Costs

The costs of calling a meeting other than by the liquidator must be deposited by the person at whose instance it is summoned, but the court or the creditors or contributories by resolution may direct payment out of the assets.

The Chairperson

The court appoints a chairperson of a court meeting. Meetings summoned

---

[6] R.S.C., Ord. 74, rr.55–83.

by a liquidator will be presided over by him or someone nominated by him. At every other meeting the chairperson shall be appointed by resolution of the meeting.

Quorum

A meeting may not act for any purpose except the election of a chairperson or the adjournment of a meeting unless there are present or represented in person three creditors entitled to vote, or in the case of a contributories' meeting, two contributories.

If the quorum is not present within 15 minutes after the time appointed for the meeting of creditors or contributories, that meeting shall be adjourned to the same day in the following week at the same time and place or such time and place as the chairperson appoints not less than seven nor more than 21 days from the date of the meeting from whence it was adjourned. Only creditors who have lodged proof of debt may vote and at meetings subsequent to the first the proof must be admitted.

Resolution

A resolution is passed by a majority in number and value, value being determined in the case of creditors by the amount of the debt and in the case of contributories by their voting rights under the articles. There is a statutory right to vote by proxy, but creditors may vote only after they have proved their debts and a secured creditor only in respect of any unsecured portion of his debt.

Proxy

General and special forms of proxy must be sent to creditors or contributories, as the case may be, with notice of the meeting; both are available only for the meeting in question or its adjournment. A person authorised to represent a company under section 139 of the Companies Act 1963 must produce to the chairperson a copy of the resolution authorising him or her either under seal or certified to be a true copy by the secretary or a director of the company.

Minutes

Minutes must be kept and must be signed by the chairperson of the meeting or next succeeding meeting. In addition a list of creditors or contributories who are present must be compiled.

26. Company Meetings in General

1. The Chairperson

The following provisions apply to the chairperson unless the articles of association state otherwise. Any chairperson elected by the members present at the meeting may be chairperson.[1] The appointment of the chairperson is regulated by the articles. The chairperson, if any, of the board of directors shall preside as chairperson at every general meeting of the company or if there is no chairperson or if he is not present within 15 minutes after the time appointed for the holding of the meeting or is unwilling to act, the directors present shall direct one of their number to be chairperson of the meeting.[2]

If at any meeting no director is willing to act as chairperson or if no director is present within 15 minutes after the time appointed for the holding of the meeting, the members present shall choose one of their number to be chairperson.[3]

The chairperson may, with the consent of any meeting at which a quorum is present, if so directed by the meeting, adjourn the meeting from time to time and place to place.[4]

At any general meeting a declaration by the chairperson that a resolution on a show of hands has been carried shall be conclusive evidence of the result.[5] Where there is an equality of votes on a show of hands or a poll, the chairperson shall be entitled to a second or casting vote.[6] The chairperson does not have a casting vote at common law; it must be given to him by the articles.[7]

Any objection as to the qualification of a voter shall be referred to the chairperson of the meeting whose decision shall be final and con-

---

[1] Companies Act 1963, s.134.
[2] ibid., Table A, art. 56.
[3] *ibid.*, Table A, art. 57.
[4] *ibid.*, Table A, art. 58.
[5] Companies Act 1963, Table A, art. 59.
[6] *ibid.*, Table A, art.61.
[7] *Nell v. Longbottom* [1894] 1 Q.B. 767.

clusive.[8] The chairperson may, with the consent of a meeting at which a quorum is present and if so directed by the meeting, adjourn the meeting.[9]

2.　Company Secretary

All companies incorporated under the Companies Acts are obliged to appoint a secretary, normally at the first meeting.[10] Any provision on the functions to be performed by a director and secretary shall not be validly satisfied if either the secretary performs the function of director and secretary at the same time or if the director performs both functions at the same time in regard to a particular matter.[11]

The directors of a public limited company must ensure that when appointing a secretary he has the requisite knowledge to discharge his function.[12] Each company shall keep at its registered office a register containing basic personal details such as name and residential address of the company secretary and of the directors.[13]

The secretary is appointed by the directors and they may impose whatever terms and conditions they may think fit.[14] The role and duties of a company secretary were described at the turn of the century as "a limited and somewhat humble character".[15] However, due to the increasing complexity of company regulation and accountability, this view cannot now be said to be an accurate reflection of the role of a company secretary, especially in larger public limited companies.

The secretary derives authority from the board of directors and in this regard the secretary has not, in the absence of authority from the

---

[8] *Wall v. London & Northern Assets Corporation* [1898] 2 Ch. 469. This authority provides a useful outline of the chairperson's powers at a company meeting.

[9] The Companies Act 1963, Table A, art. 58. For a discussion on the role of a chairperson in meetings generally. See Chap. 4. Of course, this will apply only to companies that have adopted Table A of the Companies Act 1963.

[10] The Companies Act 1963 s.175 states *inter alia*: "every company shall have a secretary who may also be one of the directors".

[11] Companies Act 1963, s.177.

[12] *ibid.*, s.236.

[13] *ibid.*, s.195.

[14] *eg. ibid.*, Table A, arts. 113–114.

[15] *George Whitechurch v. Cavanagh* [1902] A.C. 117, 124 *per* Lord Macnaghten.

board, the power to bind the company by way of contract.[16] He cannot borrow money on behalf of the company.[17] A secretary cannot convene a valid meeting at his own instance,[18] but if such notice is issued without the consent of the board, it may subsequently ratify that notice.[19]

If, following the death or resignation of a secretary, an acting secretary is appointed for a period of time, his particulars must be recorded in the register and filed with the Registrar of Companies pursuant to section 195 of the Companies Act 1963.

3. Proxies

Any member of a company entitled to attend and vote at a meeting of a company shall be entitled to appoint somebody to speak on his or her behalf and to vote on a show of hands and by poll, unless the articles provide otherwise. The proxy is not given to a member of a company not having a share capital and a member of a company shall not be entitled to appoint more than one proxy to attend on the same occasion.[20] In every notice calling a meeting of a company which has a share capital there should be a statement that a member entitled to attend and vote may appoint one or more proxies if permitted by the articles.[21]

The articles of a company may not require a proxy to be deposited more than 48 hours before the meeting or the adjourned meeting.[22] It is an offence where an invitation is issued to some members only who are entitled to vote at the company's expense.[23]

The articles of association may prescribe the style of the proxy to be used. The instrument appointing a proxy should be in writing under the hand of the appointer or of his attorney, duly authorised. If the

---

[16] *Haughton & Company v. Northard* Lowe & Wills [1928] A.C. 1.

[17] *Re Cleadon Trust Limited* [1939] Ch. 286, *per* Lord Parker "the secretary is not an official who *virtute officii* can manage all his affairs, with or without the help of servants in the absence of regular dictorate".

[18] *Re Haycroft Gold Reduction & Mining Company* [1900] Ch. 230.

[19] *Hooper v. Kerr* (1900) 83 L.T. 729.

[20] Companies Act 1963, s.136 (1).

[21] *ibid.*, s.136 (3).

[22] *ibid.*, s.136 (4).

[23] *ibid.*, s.136 (5).

appointer is a separate legal entity then it must be under seal or under the hand of an officer or attorney duly authorised.[24]

Proxies can be either general or special. In the case of a special proxy the person must have a qualification, such as being a shareholder with a right to vote. It is not necessary for the person appointed to be qualified at the time of appointment so long as he or she is appointed prior to the meeting at which the power is used.

The authority can be revoked by deposit of a later proxy, by the attendance and vote of the donor at the meeting, by the cancellation of the authority or by the death of the donor.

If a proxy form is not properly completed, the company secretary may, if time allows, send it back for amendment. However, if time does not allow or if the amended proxy forms are not received within the specified time period, the chairperson may reject such proxies. In the interests of fairness of procedure the chairperson should give his or her reason for the rejection of proxies.

A proxy holder has the right to demand or join in the demanding of a poll.[25]

4. Right to Demand a Poll

Any provision in the company articles excluding the right to demand a poll on any matter other than the election of the chairperson shall be void. The demand for a poll may be made by not less than five members having a right to vote at a meeting or by a member or members representing not less than one-tenth of the total voting rights of the members having a right to vote, or by members or a member holding shares conferring a right to vote, being shares on whichan aggregate sum has been paid up equal to not less than one-tenth of the total sum paid up on all shares conferring that right.[26]

---

[24] Companies Act 1963, Table A, art. 69.

[25] *ibid.*, s.137 (2).

[26] *ibid.*, s.137(1)(a)(b)(i), (ii), (iii).

5. Resolutions

Any resolution which is not a special resolution is an ordinary resolution. This type of resolution is the most widely used for all routine business at general meetings and also at board meetings. It is a resolution which requires a simple majority of the members entitled to vote, and actually voting, at a meeting of which proper notice has been given in accordance with the articles of association.[27] Section 133 of the Companies Act 1963 and Article 51 of Table A of the 1963 Act require that in order to validly pass an ordinary resolution at an annual general meeting it is necessary to give 21 clear days' notice to the members of the company.

If it is proposed to pass an ordinary resolution at an extraordinary general meeting and if the company is a public limited company (PLC), it is necessary to give 14 clear days' notice. If the company is a private or an unlimited company, then seven clear days' notice will suffice.

In order to prevent a sudden decision being foisted upon the members by way of ordinary resolution, the Companies Act 1963 requires a particular type of special notice in a number of instances. These include the removal of a director, pursuant to section 182 of the 1963 Act, the appointing of an auditor other than in the case of a retiring auditor, or where it is decided that such an auditor shall not be re-appointed, the removal of an auditor.[28]

Section 142 of the Companies Act 1963 provides that where special notice of a resolution is required, that resolution shall not be valid unless notice of the intention to move it has been given to the company at least 28 days before the meeting. If this cannot be done notice of the resolution should be advertised at least 21 days before the meeting.[29]

A resolution shall be a special resolution when passed by at least three-quarters of the votes cast of which 21 days' notice was given specifying the intention to propose that as a special resolution. If less than 21

---

[27] Note that in *Foss v. Harbottle* (1843) 2 Hare 461, it was established as a general principle that, where the majority passes an ordinary resolution which is within its powers to pass, the court will not usually intervene where a minority object. This of course does not entitle the majority to pass a resolution which amounts to oppression of the minority.

[28] Companies Act 1963, s.161(1)(b).

[29] *ibid.*, s.142(1). The advertisement should be given in a daily newspaper circulating in the district where the registered office of the company is situated or by any method allowed by the articles.

days' notice has been given of such a resolution, it may be proposed and passed if agreed to by the majority. However, that majority must hold not less than 90 per cent in nominal value of the shares and have a right to vote or, in the case of a company which has no share capital, they must hold not less than 90 per cent of the total voting rights of all the members.[30]

At any meeting at which a special resolution is submitted to be passed, a declaration by the chairperson that the resolution is carried shall, unless a poll is demanded, be conclusive evidence of those who voted for and against it.[31]

The terms of a resolution, special or otherwise, may be amended by ordinary resolution before a general meeting but notice must be given of the intention to amend.[32]

A resolution which is signed in writing by all the members entitled to attend and vote at a general meeting shall be as valid as if passed at a general meeting which was duly convened and held.

There are a number of situations where special resolutions may be necessary. These include:

1. to alter the objects of the company in the memorandum of association.[33]
2. to change the company's name.[34]
3. to wind up the company on a voluntary basis.[35]

A copy of each special resolution must be filed with the Registrar within 15 days after it has been passed.

A copy of every special resolution must be annexed to or incorporated in every copy of the articles issued after the passing of the resolution. Every member is entitled to a copy of the resolution subject to payment of a fee.[36]

Where a resolution is passed at an adjourned meeting of a company, the holders of any class of shares or the directors of the company, it

---

[30] Companies Act 1963, s.141(2).

[31] *ibid.*, s.141(3).

[32] *ibid.*, s.141(5).

[33] *ibid.*, s.10.

[34] *ibid.*, s.23.

[35] *ibid.*, s.251.

[36] *ibid.*, s.143(2).

shall be treated as having been passed on the date on which it was in fact passed and not on any earlier date.[37]

6. Minutes

Every company shall, as soon as practicable, cause the minutes of all proceedings of general meetings, directors' meetings and committee meetings to be entered in a book kept for the purpose.[38] Any such minute signed by the chairperson shall be evidence of the proceedings.[39] It should be noted, however, that unrecorded minutes may be proved *aliunde*.[40]

There is provision for the recording of proceedings other than in legible form if such other method of recording can be reproduced in legible form.[41] There is a right of inspection given to members and also a right to be provided with reproduction of the recording or the relevant part in legible form. When minutes are made of proceedings, those procedings shall be deemed to have been held and convened and to be proper, and all appointments of directors and liquidators valid.[42]

The minutes of the proceedings of any general meeting shall be kept at the registered office of the company and be available for inspection on request for at least two hours each day to any member. Any member, on paying a fee, is entitled to a copy.[43]

The minutes of company meetings may be kept by making entries in bound books or using another recording method.[44]

Adequate precautions must be taken against falsification of the minutes. If they are not, the company and every officer in default may be liable if prosecuted, on conviction, to a fine not exceeding £250.[45]

---

[37] Companies Act 1963, s.144.

[38] *ibid.*, s.145.

[39] *ibid.*, s.145(2).

[40] *Re Fireproof Doors* [1916] 2 Ch. 142.

[41] Companies (Amendment) Act 1977, s.4(3). This envisages the use of computerised records.

[42] Companies Act 1963, s.145(3).

[43] *ibid.*, s.146.

[44] *ibid.*, s.378(1).

[45] *ibid.*, s.378(2).

Part Seven: Conferences and Committees

27. Conferences

The organisation of a conference can be an effective way of communicating to a membership spread geographically. It is also a useful method of improving contact between the members and the leadership of an organisation, *e.g.* an executive committee and chairperson or president. It may be the only opportunity that a large number of members (or delegates representing an even wider membership) may have of meeting collectively to influence and shape the policy of an organisation.

There are, however, many variants in the organisation and purposes of conferences. There is the traditional notion of a conference, such as annual meetings of delegates of the larger national political parties, trade unions or of the leading sporting or cultural organisations in the state.

In the last decade an increasing number of national and even international conferences are being held on specific subjects or themes. These types of conference are often attended by persons who are not necessarily members of a single organisation but rather may have common professional or vocational interests such as business, medical, legal, cultural or many other interest groups. Conferences nowadays are sometimes planned and administered by professional conference organisers.

A definition of what constitutes a conference can be quite broad, encompassing a congress, consultation, convention, discussion forum, meeting, seminar, symposium, or teach-in.[1]

1. Organisation of a Conference

A conference, as we have seen, can vary in type, purpose and size and so it is difficult to list exhaustively the practical matters involved in organising such a gathering. However, there are a number of practical arrangements that the organisers would normally consider. These would include the following :

---

[1] *Diamond Thesaurus in AZ Form* (Diamond Books William Collins Sons & Co. Ltd).

Invitations

Who is to be invited and will the cost of the conference be funded wholly or partially from those who attend? The costings for the proposed conference will have to be prepared well in advance, depending on the size of the meeting. The participants, members or delegates will have to be issued with some form of identification to gain admission. This can range from a ticket or badge to full photographic and status identification. This is dictated by the size, complexity and security implications of such a gathering. There may be different categories of participant including the members or delegates, guest speakers, observers and press representatives. These different categories should ideally be identified whether by badge or in some other form.

Seating and Venue Details

The guest speakers and chairpersons for each plenary session may change for the duration of the conference and this should be taken into account.

2. Regulations Governing Conferences

This is a matter which the chairperson will have ultimate responsibility for in practice. If the chairperson is not fully aware of or familiar with his or her duties, then it may be prudent that the organiser clarifies these points. Conferences organised by large organisations will often have permanent administrative back-up which can assist the chairperson in the control of the conduct of business while in plenary session. The chair should be aware of standing orders and the organisation's constitution, if any.

Some conferences may only meet in plenary session once or twice, with the bulk of the business conducted in smaller groups. These groups will often have a mini-conference format which will need to be chaired and managed in a similar manner in terms of standing orders, length of speeches, etc.

If motions are to be voted upon in the plenary session, matters such as advance notice of motions or intention of a delegate to propose, oppose or otherwise speak on a motion, should all be clarified in advance.

Where there are no standing orders or rules dealing with such matters, the chairperson must exercise his or her discretion on such matters. However, a chairperson must act fairly and should remember that the High Court, as established under Article 34 of the Constitution, exercises a supervisory role should a decision or vote affecting, for example, a person's rights or status, be arrived at in conference in an inherently unfair manner.

The law of defamation is also a matter that should be of concern to a chairperson if a speaker appears to be making a defamatory statement. It may be prudent, for example, to intervene in a timely manner to warn the speaker to desist from making further defamatory statements.

This is not an easy matter for a chairperson to judge immediately and can be a difficult matter to make a judgment upon depending on the circumstances.[2]

A conference meeting or any meeting may be exercising a judicial or quasi-judicial function if it considers rescinding or restricting existing rights. Examples of this could be the expulsion of a member from an organisation or not allowing a voting member to attend a delegate conference.[3]

---

2 Defamation is tort [essentially a civil wrong] consisting of the publication of a defamatory statement concerning another without any just cause, whereby a person suffers injury to his or her reputation.

3 For further discussion, see Chap. 14.

28. Committees in General

The purpose for which committees are created is to enable an appointing body to delegate functions to them which would otherwise have to be dealt with by such a body. The matters delegated to a committee may be of a specialist or a routine nature.

There are a number of practical reasons for creating a committee.

1. It relieves the appointing body from having to expend time and human resources in matters which could be more efficiently dealt with by a committee.

2. The meetings of a committee are, from a practical point of view, easier to organise than would be the case in a large organisation.

3. The appointing body may appoint people with specialist knowledge in a given field to a committee as the need arises.

4. The committee system provides a useful mechanism for the purpose of carrying out research or investigation in a given area.

1.   Creation of a Committee

A committee can be formed by two different methods:

1. The first method is creation by Acts of the Oireachtas. Committees formed in this way are known as statutory committees and their terms of reference may be ascertained from the statutory instruments creating them. An example of such committees are the vocational education and county committees of agriculture.
2. The more usual method of creating a committee is by resolution of the appointing body which outlines its powers and functions, and the ambit of its duties. This is known as its terms of reference which must accurately outline what the members of the committee may or may not do.

Sometimes the standing orders of the appointing body may make provision for the conduct of the committee on such matters as the appointing of the chairperson, minutes, adjournments and the casting vote of the chairperson.

2. Approval by Appointing Body for Acts Done by the Committee

The appointing body must approve the acts of a committee in order to give them validity but such approval would not seem to be required for each step in the execution of their powers.[1] If a special requirement is specified in the giving of approval to an act, that specified requirement must be satisfied prior to the giving of an approval.[2]

Where a municipal corporation adopts a proposal of its committee, entered on its minutes under seal, that proposal must be made under the seal of such corporation or signed by a person authorised under seal by them.

In *Mayor of Kidderminster* where a contract was not under the seal of the corporation or signed on its behalf by a person authorised under seal to do so or ratified under seal, or was part performed, the contract could not be enforced.[3]

Membership of a statutory committee does not prohibit a member of a committee from resigning his position.[4]

It is noteworthy that the mere act of a committee being appointed and having powers delegated to it does not of itself deprive the appointers of their powers to act on a matter.[5]

The executive committee of a local authority was authorised to appoint sub-committees with delegated statutory powers. It appointed a number of local sub-committees to exercise powers to control the spread of rabies. As one local sub-committee had not exercised its powers the executive committee made an order itself for the muzzling of dogs in its local area. The validity of the order was challenged on the grounds that

---

[1] *Firth v. Staines.* [1897] 2 Q.B. 70.

[2] *Mayor of Oxford v. Crow.* [1893] 3 Ch. 352.

[3] *Mayor of Kidderminster v. Hardwicke* (1873) L.R. 9 Ex.13.

[4] *R. v Sunderland Corp.* [1911] 2 K.B. 458.

[5] *Huth v. Clarke* (1890) 25 Q.B.D. 391.

having delegated its powers, the executive committee could not exercise them itself.

It was held that delegation, as the word is generally used, does not imply a parting with powers by the person who grants the delegation but points rather to the conferring of an authority to do things which otherwise the person would have to do for himself. When powers are delegated to a committee, the power so conferred upon a committee consisting of several persons must be exercised by them acting in concert unless the appointing body allows delegation to one person or a sub-committee.[6]

Cook v. Ward

Three people were appointed to deal with drainage and to act in any case of emergency and to act in concert. The committee met and agreed that part of a drain should be dealt with exclusively by the defendant, a member of the committee. It was held that the committee was assuming to clothe a member of their body with a power which only the appointing board could clothe them with.

The sub-committee was not competent to delegate powers, which required the united action of all three, so the authority given to the committee had not been exercised according to the letter or spirit. Judgment was entered for the plaintiff.[7]

An appointing body may revoke or re-define the powers of the committee and also alter its membership or remove the single member.[8]

If a body has a statutory power to do something itself, a delegation of the exercise of this power to be exercised in the future would be *ultra vires*.[9]

3. Practice and Procedure at Committee Meetings

A committee will adopt its procedure according to the procedure of the appointing body, unless the appointing body lays down a certain type of

[6] *Agnew v. Manchester Corporation.*1L BR. 967.

[7] (1887) L.R. 2 C.P.D. 255. See also *D'Arcy v. The Tamar Kit Hill and Callington Railway Company* (1866) L.R. 2 Ex. 158.

[8] *Manton v. Brighton Corporation* [1951] 2 K.B.393.

[9] *Casey v. Tralee UDC* [1913] 2 I.R. 59.

procedure to be adhered to by the committee or in the case of statutory committees as specified in the statutory instrument making the appointment.

4. Quorum

Unless otherwise stated in the terms of reference or relevant statutory instrument, all members must be present to form a quorum.

5. Voting

Unless otherwise specified a majority decision will suffice.

6. Chairperson

The chairperson is appointed by the committee unless otherwise specified by the appointing body or relevant statutory instrument. The chairperson has no casting vote unless regulations provide otherwise.

7. Co-option of Members to a Committee

Members may be co-opted on to a committee unless otherwise stated by the appointing body or relevant regulations and whether such a co-opted member may vote depends on the recommendations of the appointing body.

8. Consensus of a Committee

A committee usually tries to reach a consensus on matters so as to enable it to report back to the appointing body.

9.   Terms of Reference

In order to ascertain the terms of reference of a committee, it will be necessary to look at the regulations of the appointing body or of the relevant statutory instrument.

　　If no terms exist, then the terms of reference should be laid down by the appointing body when the appointment of the committee is actually made.

10.   Minutes of Committee Meetings

Minutes are usually required in the form of minutes of the meeting tabled at a meeting of a full body, or a formal report tabled, to be considered by the full body.

11.   Accountability

The committee must account to the appointing body on all matters ranging from conflict of interest of members to financial matters.

12.   Types of Committee

Standing Committees

These are committees of a permanent nature and they deal with continuous work of the parent body. Examples of these are vocational education committees.

Special Committees/Ad Hoc Committees

These committees are appointed for a once-off occasion, usually to draw up a single report or deal with an emergency.

Committee of the Whole

This type of committee can occur when a body such as a council dissolves itself into a committee.

Executive Committees

These are committees which are given full authority to manage the affairs of the main body and an example of these would be a board of directors. This committee is still answerable to the main body from which it derives its powers.

Sub-Committees

If permitted, a committee may appoint a sub-committee to deal with specified matters.

Joint Committee

Membership is selected from two main bodies: County Councils and Corporations.

Appendices

Appendix A

Notice of an Annual General Meeting

Doolan Company Limited

Annual General Meeting

Grange Road,
Rathfarnham,
Dublin 16.

Notice is hereby given that the second annual general meeting of the said company will be held at_____ on June 16, 19__ at 12 noon for a purpose as stated hereafter.

1. To receive and consider the report of the directors and accounts for the year ended____, 19__ and to declare a dividend.

2. To elect two directors.

3. To appoint an auditor and authorise the directors to fix his remuneration.

4. To transact all further and other ordinary business of the company.

A member hereby entitled to attend and vote may appoint a proxy to attend and vote in his place and such a member shall be a member of the company.

ON BEHALF OF THE BOARD

SIGNED JOHN KELLY
SECRETARY
DATED _____

Appendix B

Notice of a Director's Meeting

Lawn Company Limited

14 Busy Lane,
Dublin 1.
Date _____

A meeting of the directors will be held at [address] on [date], at 12 noon.

BUSINESS

1. Consideration of monthly sales figures
2. Any other business

SIGNED BY _____
Secretary on behalf of the Board of Lawn Company Limited.

Appendix C

Notice of a Club Meeting

Sunny Bay Bowling Club

5 Cherrymount Hill,
Cork.

TAKE NOTICE that a monthly meeting of the club aforementioned will be held at 5 Cherrymount Hill, Cork on July 14, 19____ at 12 noon. A copy agenda is enclosed herewith.

Signed Ros Inkle
Secretary.

Appendix D

An Agenda for an Annual General Meeting of a Society

The Rose Growers' Society
Annual General Meeting

Friday June1, 19__ at 8pm at the Mariner's Hotel, The Diamond, Donegal.

AGENDA

1.   Apologies for absence

2.   Minutes of the Annual General Meeting May 31, 19__.

3.   Matters arising from the minutes.

4.   Annual accounts and treasurer's report.

5.   Possible increase of membership subscriptions.

6.   Any other business.

7.   Date of next meeting.

Appendix E

A Summary of an Agenda of a Company Annual General Meeting

Galaxy Limited

6th ANNUAL GENERAL MEETING

To be held on ___ of ___ 19___ at 12 noon at Lodgemill Hall, St Mary's Road, Limerick,

BUSINESS

1. Auditors report

2. Directors reports and accounts.

3. Declaring a dividend.

4. The election of the directors.

5. The appointment of auditors

6. Remuneration of auditors

SIGNED BY _____

Secretary on behalf of the directors of Galaxy Limited

Appendix F

A Detailed Agenda of a Company Annual General Meeting

Lagan Limited

8th ANNUAL GENERAL MEETING TO BE HELD AT RAVEN-HALL FLEET STREET, BELFAST ON MAY 1, 19__ AT 2PM

Agenda
Notes

1. The secretary to read the notice convening the meeting and also the auditors' report on the accounts

2. Requests from the meeting whether the director's report and account as printed and circulated, shall be taken as read.

3. Make statement on the company's financial position and prospects.

4. Move that the reports and accounts now before the meeting showing the company's position as at _____ be approved and adopted and that the dividend recommended by the Directors being _____% on the _____ shares [to be specified] for the year ended 19__.

5. Call on William Wafter to second the motion.

6. Put the motion to the meeting and declare the result.

7. Move motion that William Harris be elected Director of the company.

8. Call on William Wafter to second the motion.

9. Put the motion to the meeting and declare the result.

10. Move motion that William Brown be and is hereby appointed auditor of the company for one year.

11. Call on Alice Quinn to second the motion.

12. Put the motion to the meeting and declare the result.

13. Move that the remuneration of William Brown auditor of the company for the ensuing year be fixed at £_____.

14. Call on shareholders to move and second the motion.

15. Put the motion to the meeting and declare the result.

16. Special business of which notice has been given.

17. Declare that proceedings are at an end.

Appendix G

A Proxy

PROXY

READING & GREENE COMPANY LIMITED

I, Jason Gorman of Linervale in the County of Kildare being a share-holding member of Reading and Greene Company Limited do herby appoint Dawn Winter of Linden Grove, Bray in the County of Wicklow as my proxy to act and vote for me on my behalf at the Annual General Meeting of the aforesaid company to be held on the first day of June at 12 noon in the year 1998 at Linden Grove Hall, West Mall, Bray in the County of Wicklow and at any adjournment thereof signed this day of

Signed Jason Gorman.

Appendix H

Minutes of a Company Annual General Meeting

RYAN & RYAN LIMITED

Minutes of the third Annual General Meeting of the company aforementioned held on 11th day of June 1998 at 12 noon at Shamrock Hall, Brayford in the County of Wicklow.

Present in the Chair
ELIZABETH RYAN

PRESENT: Number of Directors 5
Names of Directors present:
[Insert names]

Number of members present 52

NOTICE: The Secretary Ms Burke read the notice concerning the meeting and the auditor's report.

REPORTS AND ACCOUNTS
The directors reports and accounts with the consent of the meeting have been taken as read. The Chairperson addressed the meeting and proposed that the reports and accounts now before the meeting showing the company position at the 31st December 19___ be approved and adopted.

Martin Duff seconded the motion. The motion was put to a vote at the meeting and carried unanimously.

The Chairperson then proposed that William Watt be appointed Director of the company.

The motion was seconded by Ralph Newman and carried unaminously.

The Chairperson announced that Right and Figures & Company Accountants, auditors of the company would be reappointed auditors of the company to hold office for the ensuing year.

Mr William Shilling seconded the motion which was carried unanimously.

The Chairperson announced the renumeration of Right & Figures and Company Accountants for the ensuing year to be £_____.

Mr Pound seconded the motion which was then put to a vote and carried unanimously.

SPECIAL BUSINESS

The Chairperson moved that____ and Mr Arthur seconded the motion........Etc

The final question was proposed by the Chairperson and seconded by Arthur Greene. The matter was put to a vote and declared lost on a show of hands. A poll was immediately demanded when the result of the vote was announced at the meeting by Mr William Dowd. Mr Kevin Spooner seconded the motion.

The poll was held and was carried. [Insert the votes given] The results were announced by the Chairperson.

Signed _____

Elizabeth Ryan.

Index

Index

(References are to page number)